GENDER AND MANAGEMENT ISSUES IN EDUCATION
an international perspective

GENDER AND MANAGEMENT ISSUES
IN EDUCATION
an international perspective

Edited by Pat Drake and Patricia Owen

Trentham Books

First published in 1998 by Trentham Books Limited

Trentham Books Limited
Westview House
734 London Road
Oakhill
Stoke on Trent
Staffordshire
England ST4 5NP

British Cataloguing in Publication Data
A catalogue record for this book is available from the British Library
ISBN 1 85856 087 X
HB ISBN 1 85856 118 3

Cover photograph: British Council Seminar, University of Sussex, 1996

Designed and typeset by Trentham Print Design Ltd., Chester and printed in Great Britain by The Cromwell Press Ltd., Wiltshire

DEDICATIONS

For Kitty
Pat Drake

This one is for Rosie – and for John
Patricia Owen

ACKNOWLEDGEMENTS

We should like to thank all the contributors to this volume who worked so hard, faxed and e-mailed from all over the world so that this book could come into being.

Thanks also to all the participants at the first British Council Seminar, *Gender and Management Issues in Education*, who came to Brighton in cold and snowy December 1995, and sparked off so much exciting and enlivening debate. Some of the initial themes and discussions of that week have grown and developed in the following chapters. Particular recognition goes to Heather Fitzgerald for her work in making the Seminar run so smoothly. We owe a special debt to Janet Stuart who gave us much encouragement, and to colleagues Louise Morley and Vivienne Griffiths for useful and positive advice.

We are indebted to Hayley Kirby for her intelligent and cheerful adaptation to our needs and her quick processing of so many drafts, and to Stavroula Kaldi for the index. Pat Drake would also like to record her thanks to the University of British Columbia Department of Curriculum Studies for office space, peace, quiet and computer facilities; to Margaret Cochrane and her husband Jim who made it possible for some of the writing to be completed in Canada and whose support she hopes to be able to repay someday; and to David Longman for computing advice and for taking over her teaching during the final stages of compilation. Patricia Owen would like to record her appreciation of her co-editor's tolerance and forbearance and for keeping her on target when other things got in the way. And thank you from both of us to our publisher Gillian Klein for her encouragement, helpful comments and friendly assistance with bringing this project finally to fruition.

Contents

Preface

It is appropriate that this book grew out of a shared enterprise, in more than one sense. The idea was first generated at an International Seminar organised by the British Council, of which the editors were co-directors – the first time they had undertaken such a thing.

The British Council, which exists to foster cultural and educational development in Commonwealth countries, complements aid programmes by bringing people together so that they may develop networks and plans for proposals and projects which are in the interests of development and mutual goodwill. The Council prioritises its activities in line with those of the Department for International Development (DfID).

In late 1995, amid considerable publicity, the Beijing Fourth United Conference for Women had taken place and the Platform for Action had gained a high profile. The British Council held an International Seminar: *Gender and Management Issues in Education* in Brighton, England over seven days in December 1995. It was attended by twenty-one women and four men from fifteen different countries, all of them in senior positions of management in education, as senior examinations officials, inspectors and Chief Inspectors of schools, school principals and some university lecturers. The fact that the British Council held this event, and the level of seniority of the people attracted to it testifies to the priority given to gender education. The examination of gender issues reflects the importance being attached by the major donors and development agencies to getting girls into school and keeping them there as an indicator of progress.

Academics from the University of Sussex were invited to organise the content of the Seminar and a study programme was ably put together by the Seminar Director, Dr Janet Stuart, with assistance from the editors of this book. Participants had been advised to attend the Seminar ready to contribute to one or more themes as starting points (see below). However, papers had not been seen beforehand, and so the programme was constructed according to the contributions brought by the participants. It was not possible to predict the content of the presentations, nor the direction that the discussions would take, but individuals had been invited to 'kick start' the discussions in each theme.

The themes were:

* discrimination, equal opportunities and affirmative action

* concepts of leadership; are they gender blind?

* the influence of language on gender relations

* appraisal and career development: getting to the top and working together there

* gender in the context of different cultures and religions

* making a gendered analysis of organisations

* breaking through the glass ceiling

* gender on the aid agenda of aid projects

* mentoring and networking

* action for change: planning, implementing and monitoring

* sexual harassment of young women/maternal authority of women managers

* urban/rural differences.

Each evening a report of the day was constructed which recorded the proceedings and highlighted critical issues as they arose.

A glance at the Seminar themes indicates a rather uncritical grasp of issues arising out of gender and management. To start with, the event was seen, by the organisers at least, as an opportunity for sharing ideas across countries, networking and disseminating 'good practice' or tips for dealing with discrimination against women and girls at school and at work. Whereas, because the participants held senior positions in their organisations, they were all committed to using their influence and power within the educational structures in their own countries to improve the quality of opportunity for girls and women. Thus in some ways they were already compromised, being part of that small minority which is seen, in Gordon's terms, to benefit by the reproduction of patriarchal relations through development which serve to continue to subjugate and oppress women throughout the world (Gordon, 1995). The dilemma for the Seminar participants was to understand the macro-politics of their situation whilst continuing to act micro-politically as agents for change and development. And there were differences of approach, opinion, perspective, culture, experience, age, language and resources.

> A sense of ourselves located within heterogeneous practices shows not only that we inhabit multiple and changing identities but that identities are produced and reproduced within social relations of 'race', 'gender', 'class' and sexuality. The degree to which we can work across our differences depends upon the conceptual frameworks and political perspectives from which we understand these differences. Avtar Brah (1991, p.175)

This book is in part an attempt by some of the participants in the Seminar to deal with tensions and responsibilities which arise from being female and successful. It is also an open discussion of gender and management issues in education, taking account of the nature of education as being at the same time enabling and oppressive. The book is not a compilation of the ideas discussed at the Seminar, nor a piece of theoretical rhetoric. The contributors recognise the dilemmas inherent in participating in development in their countries and are attempting to clarify some of the problematic aspects of their experience. The writers, who all have some influence and indeed power, realise that changes they are able to bring about do not solve problems but highlight even more the complexities and ambiguities of women's experience. This theme pervades the book: whether the issue is the struggle for democracy or to provide improved female access to schools; or whether it is women considering their experiences as managers in educational institutions like schools, colleges and universities.

The shared experiences of these women transcends continents: so much quickly becomes clear. With education, with work in education, as is the case when women talk about other issues common to many of their lives – for example childbirth – there is immediately recognition and mutual understanding. The power of this personal approach, this 'feminist epistemology' (see Stanley, 1990) motivated the book and continued during its production. Each contributor has reworked her chapter at least once, following an editorial critique on first drafts along lines of: 'avoid sweeping generalisations', 'try not to be too anecdotal', 'provide evidence for your assertions' etc. We were forcibly reminded of our duty to allow each individual story to be told during this process when one of the authors, Venitha Soobrayan replied:

> Thank you for your constructive comments... there are some issues I would like to comment on. I refer to your point that the draft reads as 'very anecdotal' and I should 'legitimate my personal account'... How does one legitimate personal experience? Why is it not legitimate? Will it become legitimate if I found a similar experience recorded in a text? ...One of the central points raised by women writers is that personal experience ought to be a valid basis for discussion...

There were further issues which the editors were unable to ignore. Another contributor wrote:

> Thank you very much for your help with the sentences, tenses, etc., which I appreciate very much because English certainly is not my native language. However, is there anything wrong with using expressions which are not used in English? ...Actually, now that you tell me I can't help thinking that it *might* give the article (sic) a kind of (strange, if you wish) charm, because it is written for a foreigner.

So there were some difficult decisions to be made (as there always are) about the processes of editing. While trying to keep to what we felt to be the bare meaning of the authors' original text, the editors, as mother tongue speakers of English, have nevertheless changed the syntax, phraseology, and sometimes whole paragraphs, to make all of it easily understood.

We hope that in the process we have not distorted or misrepresented anything the contributors were wishing to convey, or compromised the ideas they have put forward.

Not all the writers of the following chapters were involved in the Seminar; similarly not all the participants in the Seminar chose to contribute to the book. However, discussion and sharing of common themes helped to bring the pieces in this book into being. Shared work has also been a thread running through the process of compiling and editing, as well as contributing to, this book. Although based in the same institution (the University of Sussex Institute of Education), the editors found themselves, particularly in the later stages of the book's construction, having to collaborate and liaise on putting it together while working thousands of miles apart and living in a succession of different countries. We could only 'speak' to each other in writing, via machines. The luxury of hurried conversation in the corridor; leisurely discussion of a section over coffee; the immediate response of one of us to a comment made by the other; reading body language; detecting difficulties; encouraging the other after a heavy day; small acts of protection for each other against external incursions on precious writing time: all these were denied. We realised that, with the benefits of close contact removed, we had to function in different ways. The difficulties familiar to all academics, of finding usable spans of uninterrupted thinking and writing time, were compounded for us by the need to communicate across time zones: our e-mail 'conversations' could only take place – usually by appointment – when one of us started work at the crack of dawn while the other stayed up late.

Most of the contributors to the book sent their papers and letters to us by electronic means, and editorial comment and query was returned in a similar way. This made it possible for a truly international volume to be created by women living and working thousands of miles apart. And the importance for all writers, especially women writers, of being willing to use electronic communication as a tool to forward their work should never be underestimated. Dale Spender has argued that the new electronic media have created unimaginable opportunities in the area of education and authorship which we must learn to use for good.

> We should never lose sight of the fact that even as we talk of the democratisation of authorship, we are speaking of First World societies and highly privileged communities. (Spender, 1995 p86)

We felt it important that we should assert our right to make the electronic media work for us and we hope we have done so effectively.

However, the voices of all the women writing in this book speak for themselves, and we are proud that they come across so clearly. We hope that this book will open views in new directions: in the manner in which it was created by the many writers whose ideas it presents; in the way we as editors have put it together; in the challenge it poses to some aspects of educational hegemony; and in the ideas we hope it will help to generate about gender and management issues in education from a truly international perspective.

Pat Drake
Patricia Owen
June 1997

Notes and References

Brah, A. (1991) 'Questions of Difference and International Feminism' in Aaron, J and Walby, S (1991) (eds) *Out of the Margins: Women's Studies in the Nineties*. Lewes: Falmer.

Gordon, Rosemary (1995) *Causes of Girls' Academic Under-achievement: the Influence of Teachers' Attitudes and Expectations on the Academic Performance of Secondary School Girls*. Occasional Papers Number 8, March 1995. HRRC at the Faculty of Education, University of Zimbabwe.

Spender, D. (1995) *Nattering on the Net: Women, Power and Cyberspace*. Melbourne, Spinifex.

Stanley, L. (1991) 'Feminist Auto/Biography and Feminist Epistemology' in *Out of the Margins: Women's Studies in the Nineties*, op. cit.

The Contributors

Lynn Davies is Professor of International Education in the School of Education, University of Birmingham. She has taught at primary, secondary and tertiary level in the UK, Mauritius and Malaysia, as well as doing consultancy work in a range of developing countries. Her teaching and research interests are in educational management internationally, with a particular focus on equity, democracy and deviance. She has written books and articles on women and educational management, and on the relationship between school effectiveness and democracy. Her latest book (with Clive Harber) is *School Management and Effectiveness in Developing Countries: the post-bureaucratic school* (Cassell, 1997). She is Convenor of the Institute for Democracy in Education, and Chair of the British Council Task Force on Gender and Development.

Pat Drake is a lecturer at the University of Sussex Institute of Education. At the time of the Gender and Education Seminar she was Director of the post-graduate secondary initial teacher training programme at Sussex. Her background is in mathematics education and she develops curriculum materials which tackle themes of gender and mathematics in the workplace. Her experience of directing the teacher preparation programme at a time of transition in Britain into a functional, centralised government-driven professional preparation was greatly enhanced by her research work with her colleague Lisa Dart into aspects of mentoring as a model for inducting teachers. Pat has direct experience of educational systems in England and Wales, Malawi, South Africa, Zimbabwe and Canada.

Devarakshanam Betty Govinden is Head of the Department of Curriculum Studies, Faculty of Education, at the University of Durban-Westville (UDW), South Africa. She is also seconded as a special assistant to the Rectorate at UDW. Her academic work includes research on feminist and gender issues in literature, literary theory, critical pedagogy, multiculturalism, educational management and theology. At present she is working on identity politics, the education of girls and women in south africa, and women, gendered organisational culture and management.

Chrysanti Hasibuan-Sedyono's first careers were with Uniliver and later Richardson Vicks Indonesia where she has had various positions in marketing management. When she felt that her brands were competing with her children for her attention, Chrysanti joined the Institute for Management Education and Development (LPPM), where her expertise in marketing management, international business negotiations and cross cultural communications go a long way. She has also been very involved in the UNDP and World Bank projects for Indonesian exporters. Her present position is Assistant to the President for External Relations. Having personally gone through all the inner conflicts and soul searching faced by a traditional woman with a successful career, Chrysanti became interested in the issues facing women managers. Hence, despite her economics and international management background, she has been indulging herself in studying, speaking and writing about women in management.

Fiona Leach is a senior lecturer in International Education at the University of Sussex Institute of Education. She has extensive work experience on British-funded educational projects in Africa. Her current professional and academic interests are: gender, education and development, women and the labour market, the cross-cultural transfer of knowledge and skills, international development assistance to education, project management and implementation.

Jeanette Morris is a lecturer in the School of Education, Faculty of Humanities and Education at the University of the West Indies, St. Augustine, and former coordinator of the Women and Development Studies programme. She teaches methodology in the curriculum area of Modern Languages and lectures in the Sociology of Education. Her research interests relate mainly to gender issues in education and she is currently pursuing doctoral studies in the area of women and educational management, with an emphasis on the careers of female administrators.

Patricia Owen lectures in Education at the University of Sussex. She teaches on teacher preparation and Masters programmes in Education, and has developed links and exchanges with several European partner institutions. She is also investigating aspects of educational provision in India. Together with Vivienne Griffiths, she has written on partnership schemes with schools in initial education of teachers. An historian by training, and an active member of the UK Women's History Network, she is particularly interested in the lives and achievements of women teachers, the development of curriculum materials which acknowledge women's contributions to past societies and the connections between school-taught history and the development of school students' ideas about democracy and gender.

Zeeshan H. Rahman was born in Dhaka, Bangladesh. After completing her Bachelors and Masters in Public Administration from the University of Dhaka, she started her career in the Bangladesh Rural Advancement Committee (BRAC). Since then she has been involved in developing materials for 35,000 non-formal schools where 70 per cent of the students are girls. Currently, she is working as a Materials Developer Specialist in the Materials Development Unit of the Non-Formal Primary Education Programme. She has written several story books, textbooks and teachers' manuals for these schools. She is also a core member of the Woman's Advisory Committee of BRAC.

Venitha Soobrayan is a lecturer at the Springfield College of Education in Durban, South Africa. She teaches English language and literature to pre-service and in-service students. She serves on the editorial committee of the only feminist journal in the country – *Agenda*. She says:

> My greatest joy is my little daughter who is almost one and who finds her own way of telling me her story everyday. Of course she constantly tests my theories of gender. I feel very lucky to have a rewarding family and work life.

Chapter 1

INTRODUCTION
Gender, Management and Education:
an international perspective
– hero(ines) and villains

Pat Drake and Patricia Owen

There are heroines and villains[1] in every classroom, staffroom and ministry of education. It's time the heroines were recognised. That this book exists is a statement about global interest in the condition of the world's women and about many of those women becoming increasingly involved in positions from which they are able to assert some influence over future events. Women are leaders and, sometimes in the same countries, women are amongst the most oppressed people. In 'developing' countries particularly, that is countries which are largely dependent on world aid, women are cast as both bringers of change and guardians of the old cultures. Traditionally and universally, women are seen as the main nurturers of the young, and from this role follows their 'natural' involvement with education. It is considered important to educate women in order to bring about the advances which will supposedly improve the economic health of developing countries and the living conditions of those who inhabit them. It is also through women that family 'values' and traditions are transmitted. Sometimes these two missions lie uneasily together.

Yet while emphasis on women and issues which affect and are affected by them grows, global developments in the 1980s and 90s bring ever greater variation in the conditions of the world's women: for many, things are getting worse.

The last quarter of the twentieth century has seen major pressures on even the world's strongest economies, along with fundamental political upheavals and realignment. Following the end of the Cold War, the erstwhile superpowers face growing demands on the diminishing funds available for international assistance. The appearance of new and often European claims on western aid budgets has possibly diverted attention away from needy economies in the 'older' developing regions such as Africa.

In some former Eastern bloc countries, adopting or re-learning un-accustomed 'real' forms of democratic government and the re-establishment of independent status and assertions of autonomy has menaced regional, if not international, peace. Unfamiliar exposure to the realities of 'free for all' market economies exacerbate threats to stability. At the same time, in East Central Europe, women are finding rights given from above in the past '... are taken away by market and 'new' ideological pressures' (Einhorn, 1993 p257).

In the world's agricultural economies, survival depends upon hard work, incessant family effort, unsophisticated use of resources, often con-siderable reliance upon moneylenders and loans and luck with climatic conditions. Protracted negotiations at international level affect and delay the liberalisation of trade in agricultural products, with serious repercussions for such rural economies: the trend towards formation of trading blocs such as the European Community also threatens diversity of trading agreements and consequent deterioration in terms of trade. Large-scale international debts hang around the necks of many of the world's poorest countries, along with deteriorating infrastructures as budget deficits grow. Furthermore, the urgent demands of the north – Europe, Japan, North America – for cheap material goods, whether sportsgear, clothing or microchips, have led to the mobilisation in parts of Asia and the Far East of a huge compliant labour force, generally women and children, facing desperate individual debts, working in appalling conditions and for bare subsistence wages – which the con-sumers of the goods they produce no doubt imagine to have disappeared with the demise of the nineteenth century.

Elsewhere, especially in some parts of Africa, the breakdown of the old certainties of cold war confrontation and the concomitant withdrawal of superpower shoring-up of rulers and power blocs have added further uncertainties and disastrous instability to the already divisive consequences of colonialism. Chronic social and economic crises flare up, and inevitably the first and most piteous victims are women and children; western television screens are quick to show pictures of helpless women pushed to ultimate deprivation and despair by a crisis, be it war or famine, which their country is powerless to alleviate.

However, advancements in the condition of women have been made, and not just in the 'developed' countries of the north and west, where legislation appears – not always justifiably – to protect and guarantee their rights. Developing countries have set and progressed towards targets which increase women's representation at all but the highest levels of government, administration and public sector services. In Zimbabwe, for example, a target to increase the number of women at all levels of the Civil Service to 33 per cent by the year 2000 has been made possible by abandoning an old principle of seniority, whereby promotion was automatically considered first for those with most experience at the previous rung of the promotion ladder. This new strategy enabled women to rise through the ranks, overtaking men in some cases many years their senior. However, economic restructuring demanded by aid donors and the World Bank in developing countries where debts were increasing, has closed the door on some of these manifestations of equity and justice. Rationalisation of civil services, reducing the numbers of jobs in government administrations and bureaucracies, also slows down women's advancement while not necessarily achieving the goal of streamlining procedures. In any case, equal pay regulations and conditions of service, e.g. provision and time for breastfeeding in the workplace, apply only to the relatively small number of professional women.

At the bottom of the educational ladder, it is proving difficult to persuade girls to complete secondary education in order to gain access to further education and training. Data from Malawi, Zimbabwe and Ghana (Swainson, 1996), show that girls are not completing secondary schooling. In these poorest economies, education of girls competes with the need for domestic labour. Add to this the dangers of exposing girls at school to sexual harassment and risk of pregnancy from teachers and male pupils (Gordon, 1995, Hyde and Kadzamira, 1994), and the likelihood of failure in extremely competitive, expensive norm-referenced examinations[2] and a picture emerges of huge differences between the educated and privileged, who go on to become leaders and innovators, and those who are as oppressed as ever by lack of opportunity.

Nevertheless, the economic empowerment of women through education and business opportunity is seen as the way forward to stronger, healthier developed nations.

> ...The evidence of significant returns to female education includes reduced fertility, reduced infant and maternal mortality, enhanced family health and welfare, improved children's education, and increased agricultural productivity, earnings and overall economic productivity for women and the larger economy. (Odaga and Heneveld, 1995, p2)

However, business opportunities for women depend on access to loans and credit. All too frequently, women are seen as tied to traditional activities which generate little economic or cultural independence. In an interesting analysis of this position, Gordon (1996) argues that research and discussion on gender issues have been informed by what she terms a *modernising* perspective, one from which education is seen relatively unproblematically as the major emancipating mechanism for women. Through this approach it is possible to ignore and exclude an analysis of education as yet another dimension to cultural imperialism. The oppression of women is explained as a consequence of 'stubborn and enduring aspects of traditional cultures', which persist despite the best modernising attempts to overcome them. She writes:

> The nature of the state, whether colonial or post-colonial, is not taken into consideration: the state is comprehended as a neutral institution. In particular with regard to the post-colonial state, politics and economics are separated and the post-colonial state is presented as politically autonomous. The dependence of the post-colonial state on foreign capital is not seen as problematic. (Gordon,1996, p216)

Gordon claims that the state, with apparent ease, creates systems which exploit and subordinate women across class, race, cultural and national boundaries, serving the interests of patriarchy in both the developed and the underdeveloped world. Education, she suggests, is such a system.

This is a perspective through which the donor programmes in the developed world and their priorities for funding may be considered. The British government has an extensive aid programme, managed through the Department for International Development (DfID). Other developed countries also contribute to economic development through loans (e.g. Sweden, Canada, Germany), as does the World Bank and organisations for development projects and initiatives[3], such as UNICEF.

We are aware that the very existence of this book salutes the dominant discourse which requires a written object to give ideas and stories legitimation and currency. There is also the prevailing climate in universities which requires academics to publish as much as possible in order to maintain a high international reputation, for with that comes more research funding. That this book could probably not have been produced outside the ambit of the British aid programme and will contribute to academic standing is to make one point at the expense of another. Women are easily caricatured as either 'victims' of circum- stances or 'villains' who contribute to the oppression of others. The truth is more complicated. All people are positioned by circumstances, and we all have to earn a living, look after families, feed and clothe ourselves and others.

Our contribution is, we hope, to bring to public attention the realities and practicalities and concerns of women who, if defined as managers, whilst possibly taking an active part in structural systems which oppress other women, are able to comment from a standpoint of practical and professional knowledge about issues of education and gender.

'Education' and 'gender' are not simple, one-dimensional terms; each carries a wealth of definitions and interpretations, some of which pre- dominate here. Schools can be democratic or hierarchical, they can teach girls about their expected place in society, their future role as citizens, as well as how to read, write, count, and how to pass or not pass or even enter examinations. They can provide a setting in which women, as teachers, managers or administrators, can develop careers or remain at a lowly, servicing level.

Education is not only located in schools. In Universities, as much as in reading or study circles for adults who never attended formal classes as children, similar issues arise. Finding out about one's own capabilities and developing self-knowledge is just as much an outcome of education as systematic instruction in particular subjects, at whatever academic level. In the contributions to this book, the concept of 'education' is explored in all these contexts, as it interacts with other themes.

'Gender' is one of the threads which runs right through every chapter. 'Oh well', as a colleague opined: 'that means women, doesn't it?' Well, yes and no. Analysis based on gender seeks to do more than chronicle the experiences of women: inequities between being male and female are also examined. Contributors to this book examine power relations within organisations; choices men and women make in terms of how they plan or are unable to plan their lives, education and careers; characteristics of men and women when they aspire to or assume significant roles within the 'education' world in whichever country. Women and men are generally expected, or conditioned, to have attributes, attitudes or responses specifically *because* they are men or women. Because one of these is that men are expected to be more appropriate managers, any consideration of gender issues is likely to highlight problems for women; whether it is the women themselves or the difficulties they face that are seen as the 'problem'. And while men generally remain in the majority of the powerful positions in education, as in other organisations, this will tend to continue.

But men can be the 'victims' as well as the 'villains', and definitions of 'gender' issues in the chapters which follow make this clear. Structures and delivery of education systems are distorted, and therefore flawed, if they only take account of the talents and the needs of one half of humanity.

The theme of 'management' used here thus encompasses the viewing of management as a concept and also the particular characteristics of women as managers. 'Management styles' and the nature of 'leadership' are unpacked, raising the question of whether there really is, or can be, a 'neutral' form of management or whether management *must* be gendered. Women managers, whose success (if achieved) is examined here, are presented in their particular context and the construct of the 'career woman' is investigated. What kind of manager is she? In whose interest does she exist? Would it be a good thing for educational organisation if there were many more of her, at every level? What qualities are managers, women and men, expected to demonstrate; what social expectations, prejudices and stereotypes come into play? Does the definition of a 'good' manager shift when a woman does the job?

The international dimension to the book adds clarity and insight to these issues because we can all contrast the contexts described with our own experiences. The authors come from Bangladesh, Britain, Indonesia, South Africa and the West Indies, all very different geographically and providing contrasting political regimes. There are some surprising similarities between women managers in Indonesia and those in the West Indies. It is interesting that the notion of leadership becomes problematised in the emerging democracy of South Africa. It is a challenge to UK readers to find that an organisation in Bangladesh is more gender-sensitised than say a British university, even without the support of equal opportunities legislation. We question the concept of development: developing countries are in receipt of aid and are therefore required to prioritise according to donor priorities; their aim is to develop sustainable economies. Education is such a priority, particularly the education of girls, yet we see how this cannot be done by half measures; educating girls requires a radical overhaul of the entire educational and political infrastructure. Education affects work and society and vice versa. We wonder to what extent this has been achieved in developed countries of the North and West; Britain, North America, and Japan.

The contributors are all speaking about the world as they see it. This sense of autobiography is especially powerful because although they come from different countries, the issues raised are instantly recognisable and relevant to all women. As editors we have done our best to allow the ideas and stories of the contributors to speak as clearly as possible.

The book is arranged in three sections: *Equity and Democracy; Schooling and Work; Women as Managers*, with a linking section to introduce each. We work from a broad political perspective at the beginning of the book towards more intimate personal accounts of authors' research at the end of it. Throughout, the emphasis is on relating the different dimensions of educational experience from a 'genderless' as well as a female perspective, taking as a starting point the school and those who might go to it, as well as work in it, through to the structure which provides the educational opportunity and policy formulations. Each section offers a chapter providing analytical overview, plus one or two case studies from different countries, allowing readers to recognise and generalise the issues.

The first section: *Equity and Democracy* deals with concepts of management and leadership in a democratised world, and debates the gendering of these concepts within political climates. The second section: *Schooling and Work* considers the interaction between gender in schools and gender in vocational settings, especially in the context of donor programmes in developing countries. In the third section: *Women as Managers*, women managers' experiences in three different parts of the world are considered: in Indonesia, the West Indies and South Africa. The style here is auto-biographical and the women's stories are told largely in their own words.

The book calls for action. Examining gender issues and good practice for women in education is good practice for education. The conclusion summarises questions raised implicitly in the book, indicating ways forward for the increasingly vocal international groups who recognise that for education to become a truly transformational tool it cannot continue to transmit values which reproduce the *status quo*. The world is not static. It needs more and more individual heroines to rout the villains in classrooms, staffrooms and education departments across the world, to take power and relay it effectively. And it needs all of us who are involved in eduation and education management and who question the current gendered state of affairs to set about reconstructing the concept of education in any way we can.

Notes

1. *Eds*: thanks to Lynn Davies for this image.

2. Norm-referenced examinations are designed so that results fit a 'normal' or Gaussian distribution, often referred to as a bell-shaped curve. The pass mark is arbitrarily assigned so that a fixed proportion of the candidates pass the examination and a proportion must fail. This means that the most poorly schooled individuals bolster the achievements of the better educated. Norm referenced examinations suit societies divided by race or class or gender very well, as they act as a filter through which only the privileged few may pass. There is also an entry fee so, regardless of who passes or fails, the examination boards are able to profit — yet again at the expense of the poorest people, those for whom the outlay on examination fees, especially for girls, is an expense they can ill afford.

3. That this aid is linked directly to economic policy in developing countries is unquestionable. As I write (April 1997), in the newspaper in Harare is the headline 'Britain to cancel $280 million debt'. This, one reads, is provided 'Zimbabwe comes up with a sound programme of action *acceptable to donors* (my emphasis added) to reform the economy under the second phase of the liberalisation process started in 1991.'

References

Einhorn, B. (1993) *Cinderella Goes to Market: Citizenship, Gender and Women's Movements in East Central Europe.* London: Verso.

Gordon, R. (1995) *Causes of Girls' Academic Underachievement: the Influence of Teachers' Attitudes and Expectations on the Academic Performance of Secondary School Girls.* Occasional Papers Number 8, March 1995. HRRC at the Faculty of Education, University of Zimbabwe.

Gordon, R. (1996) Legislation and Educational Policy in Zimbabwe: the state and reproduction of patriarchy, in *Gender and Education* Vol. 8 No. 2 pp 215-229 1996.

Hyde, K.A.L. and Kadzamira, E.C. (1994) *GABLE, Knowledge, Attitudes and Practice Pilot Survey.* Report, Centre for Social Research, University of Malawi, Zomba.

Odaga, A. and Heneveld, W. (1995) *Girls and Schools in Sub-Saharan Africa: From Analysis to Action.* World Bank Technical Paper No. 298. Washington DC: World Bank

Swainson, N. (1996) *Redressing Gender Inequalities in Education: A Review of Constraints and Priorities in Malawi, Zambia and Zimbabwe.* Report to The British Development Division in Central Africa of the Overseas Development Administration.

Section One
Equity and Democracy

In this section, the concept of management and the concept of leadership are explored within the context of democratic frameworks for education establishments. Lynn Davies argues that a truly democratic organisation is the only environment in which management can be effectively gender-sensitive. Yet the example provided by Venitha Soobrayan illustrates that whilst a democracy might be a necessary condition for equitable management structures, it is not sufficient to guarantee them.

Venitha Soobrayan argues that leadership is a gendered concept, from the stance of someone who was rather surprised to find that she was one of a minority who thought so at the British Council Brighton Seminar. This view was controversial, with most of the seminar participants believing that it was the leader who determined the values associated with that position. Coming from South Africa, Venitha is aware that the struggle to establish democracy may not actually be advancing the cause of women beyond token representation. She uses what she sees and hears happening in public at government level in South Africa to probe the context of education, and she presents a cogent argument which draws upon politics, management style, characteristics of leaders, language and power relations to make her case.

Lynn Davies maintains from her own research and that of others, that individual male and female leaders are not characterised differently. Men and women have similar aspirations and concerns: for themselves; their families; their conditions of service, and so on. It is the nature and structure of the organisation they work in which dictates and permits advancement within it – or not as the case may be. The organisation, be it school, aid agency, government department or non-governmental organisation, has responsibility for providing a structure which allows employees to develop professionally. Here, it is argued, is the place for research, for people to understand the extent to which their organisation is truly democratic. She explains bureaucracy so as to distinguish between 'weak' and 'strong' democracies. Bureaucracies are hierarchies – and Lynn Davies shows how the 'weak' and the 'strong' each gender the workplace by different means.

The two chapters show us how, in these hierarchies generated through 'weak' democracy, education management discourse is peppered with linguistic references which help to construct the notion of effective leadership and, with it, power and control. The world of sport provides a rich source for metaphors for teamwork, which in such a context is usually posed in opposition to competitiveness: 'pulling together', 'moving the goalposts', 'pulling no punches', and so on. Whilst it is possible to argue that women are involved in activities where this language would be recognised, it is also true to say that activities (for example making a patchwork quilt) which depend upon teamwork without competition, and which incidentally are recognisably female, do not appear in the discourse. Metaphors are also drawn from military and sexual contexts, and it is here that language of dominance, control and oppression becomes explicit.

The example provided by Venitha Soobrayan from South Africa also illustrates how advice to school principals in management textbooks still in use is old-fashioned, relying on outdated notions of efficiency, time-management, speediness and sense of separateness from employees. These texts probably reflect the assumptions prevailing at the time they were written; in South Africa, apartheid was predicated on a social hierarchy. That advice from these tomes is still in circulation makes it especially important for women to challenge and question the practices within their organisations; not only are old practices unacceptable in the new South Africa but the advice itself seems contrary to preferred styles of working of many women and men.

Taken together, the chapters provide a powerful and insightful discussion of issues surrounding organisations and the way they work. The combined critique of the *status quo* offers the possibility of alternatives, which, it is argued, women and men must consider if they are going to make the workplace a just place for people to be.

Chapter 2

Democratic practice, gender and school management

Lynn Davies

Introduction

The novelist Anita Brookner commented on the fable of the tortoise and the hare:

> In real life, of course, it is the hare who wins. Every time. Look around you. And in any case it is my contention that Aesop was writing for the tortoise market... Hares have no time to read. They are too busy winning the game. (*Hotel du Lac*, 1984)

When we talk about gender and management, this is really code for women and management, or more precisely, getting more women into management. It is seen as turning tortoises into hares, or finding some mechanism by which the female tortoise can surprise everyone by out-performing the male hare. The problem with the books on women and management are that they are written for the tortoise market. They are often about women competing in a man's world, eyeing up the hurdles and sneaking through into the winning box. Few men read these books. Few men will read this one. And so they carry on winning.

This chapter argues that we need to reconceptualise the problem. Para-doxically, the way to achieve a better gender 'balance' and a more feminised management of education is to stop focusing on women, or even gender, directly. Instead, the focus should be on management, now it is conceived and how it operates. I look at contemporary discourses in organisations, and how they share hierarchy. I contrast this with inter-national notions of 'good governance'. My argument is that the 'women problem' is a problem of democracy, and that a solution to gender and indeed other forms of inequity or injustice is to strive for more democratic educational institutions.

This standpoint is the result of a number of false starts in quite a long trail examining women and educational management in an international context. I started in the early eighties by examining whether females in developing countries were 'under-represented' in educational management. Statistics were hard to come by, but the patterns of fewer women as seniority increased seemed to be common to a number of countries. To see whether the reasons were also similar, I designed questionnaires for distribution to teachers in some African countries where I had contacts. These asked about domestic constraints, about career perceptions, about experiences of being interviewed and so on. Some interesting data about their lives emerged, but also a realisation of the imperialistic nature of many of the questions I asked. In systems where teachers do not apply for jobs, but are transferred or – if fortunate – just promoted, then questions about career planning and about job interviews are inappropriate. The only really conclusive finding was that women teachers spent more time on domestic duties than male teachers – hardly an earth-shattering discovery, and about as useful as establishing that taller men wear longer trousers.

I was also starting to be concerned about the dilemmas involved in such a research project, in terms of exploiting Third World women for *my* data, for *my* career enhancement (Davies, 1987). The next move therefore was to involve colleagues elsewhere, and to design research which provided the opportunity for self-reflection and self-development for those completing it. As with an appraisal interview, the questionnaire asked people to reflect on what they had achieved, what their aspirations were, and what might prevent them from achieving their goals. I asked them to indicate what they wanted from their organisation, their managers, their colleagues; I also asked what duties they did in the school. The final section asked about home life, their aspirations in that context, and the intersection of home with work. This 'self-appraisal schedule' was completed by a sample of teachers from five African countries, Malaysia and Hong Kong; a Sri Lankan colleague simultaneously used the schedule to provide an in-depth case study of her country.

In designing the questionnaire and accompanying interviews, I was still firmly locked into traditional 'sex differences' research, and had hoped to find significant differences between female and male teachers in their career history and in the way that they saw work, or home, or the organisation, or self. The reality was not so simple and, initially, it was disappointing. There did not seem to be much difference in 'career aspiration' – age was a better predictor, or, in countries like Sri Lanka, the degree of instability in the political system and social unrest which would affect people in planning their lives. Nor were there marked gender differences in qualification level or previous experience. Apart from the traditional domestic science versus technology split, there was possibly less stereotyping of subject roles than in many Western contexts.

The 'dual-role' thesis also took some knocks. There were no significant sex differences in perceptions of a conflict between home and school. Both sexes placed 'improved child care', 'parental leave if a child is sick' and 'responsibility leave for care of relatives' at the bottom of a longish list of ways to integrate work and personal life. They were more attracted by such areas as a life skills or personal development course, or by clear specifications of school jobs and duties. The results of this project and our hypotheses to explain the findings are written up fully in *Women and Men in Educational Management: An International Inquiry* (Davies and Gunawardena, 1992). Men and women appeared to want the same things from the organisation, such as constructive criticism, recognition for doing a good job, social contact with colleagues and efficient administration that made their work smooth. Girls are often supposed to choose teaching because it is a nice job which will fit in with family life. Contrary to this myth, we found that women did not primarily enter teaching for the short hours and long holidays (myths in themselves in some parts). Interestingly, neither sex seemed to put 'participation in management' as a high priority, an initial puzzle for us, although more men than women described management as a 'duty' for them.

The most convincing 'sex differences' which did emerge from the research were that:

- men performed more of the administrative tasks in school in general

- men assumed in particular more of the 'hard' and visible managerial tasks which anticipate public decision-making

- men were more confident (or arrogant?) about their capacity to do managerial tasks, *whether or not they actually performed them*

- In some of the men, there was a dominant discourse which stressed competition, material reward, and status.

What was starting to emerge were not so much broad 'gender roles' but that actual workings of institutions allowed the management discourse to be 'captured' by a certain group of men who saw life in competitive, hierarchical and status terms. They talked about their classes winning various competitions; their aspirations were to be 'top' – to be a head, or senior in the Ministry. This had emerged too from the pilot study, where a man's hope could be expressed as 'to get to number one in my subject and the country'. There certainly were not enough jobs to go round for the number of men who wanted to be Director of Education. Even in their home life, they wanted: 'a home that is the envy of others'. For the unmarried men, getting wives was an important career move to give them status, support and stability; unmarried women on the other hand were more likely to cast impending marriage as a potential threat to career. For some men, home and work present little psychological conflict, because the desire for high remuneration, for conspicuous consumption by family and hence the need for managerial status all combine to urge them onwards. It is less that men actually want to 'manage' as such, but that they incline to the prestige or reward that public duty provides. Female ambitions and achievement – and those of some other men – were cast more in terms of how much their classes had learned, and a sense of satisfaction for a job well done. Many women did not want to move away from their colleagues by being promoted.

The conclusions of the study were that the hierarchical, competitive nature of management in schools, and the capturing of the management discourse by one version of masculinity were the root problems. The aim of equity for teachers should not be 'entryism' – getting more women into management – but challenging our existing concepts of how schools should be run, and in whose interests. Many men are also disadvantaged and frustrated by the typical bureaucratic pyramid in the conventional way of seeing workplaces and rewards for work. More importantly, pupils are also disadvantaged by this. The reward for good teaching is often to leave the classroom and enter the hallowed portals of management. There is no guarantee that good teachers make good administrators, nor that women managers necessarily bring superior styles with them. Women can be just as authoritarian or bureaucratic as men, and single-sex girls' schools can be just as rigid and opaque as single-sex boys' schools. We are looking for structures which enable good teachers to stay teaching and yet get recognition and reward; which enable full participation in decisions, by staff or students; and which prevent discrimination in terms of who assumes which sorts of power and authority. This is democracy.

Discourses of dominance and bureaucracy

Before making an argument for democracy, and how it might be achieved, it is necessary to consider whether existing forms of management are fundamentally 'gendered', that is, sexist, or whether management itself is neutral, but just has more men in it. This involves looking at 'discourse' within organisations. Discourse is language linked to the use of power, which creates and sets limits to the 'truths' by which we can understand our world. The opposition of 'man' and 'woman', and the understandings attached to these terms, is a key discourse. The use of language is central to 'hegemony', which refers to dominance by apparent consent rather than force, by the successful diffusion of ideas, values and social 'rules'. A discourse which posits the male as dominant and aggressive does not always advantage men: research on masculinity in schools shows boys as limited and constrained by such discourses, finding difficulty in expressing alternative versions of masculinity (Mac an Ghaill, 1994).

If we look at management discourses in schools, we find that many hark back to military or colonial times. The emphasis is on obedience to rules and on unquestioned discipline, as is appropriate in a war or competitive sporting setting. As I illustrate in my book *Beyond Authoritarian School Management* (Davies, 1994), headteachers will talk of 'steering a tight ship', 'marshalling the troops, 'patrolling the corridors'. The operation is that of guerrilla warfare, with teachers and heads having constantly to be vigilant. Similarly, sporting discourses stress team playing, goal scoring, 'healthy competition', 'level playing fields' and 'moving the goalposts'. This sounds softer than the military, but still carries the implication of beating the enemy, of another team to conquer. It is fascinating how far we have come to accept this argot, so that education as competition (between pupils, between schools) is the taken-for-granted driving force.

Discourses of dominance are allied to bureaucratic modes of operation. Schools the world over show features of typical bureaucracies, demonstrating both vertical and horizontal divisions (Harber, 1989; Davies and Harber, 1997). The most simple definition of bureaucracy is Scott's 'the existence of some kind of specialised administrative staff' (1981, quoted in Ianello, 1992). However, bureaucracy as an organising form contains a number of essential characteristics surrounding this specialism, most commonly analysed through Max Weber's list of features: staff members are personally free, observing only the impersonal duties of office; there is a clear hierarchy of offices; the functions of office are clearly specified; officials are selected on qualification and merit; salary is graded according to position in the hierarchy; the official's post is his or her sole major occupation; there is a career structure, with promotion possible either by seniority or merit, according to the judgement of superiors; the official is subject to a unified control and disciplinary system (Albrow, 1970). Thus in a 'pure' bureaucracy, activities and roles are separated according to job descriptions and specialisations; decisions are made by virtue of one's position and level within the structure. Activities are circumscribed by rules and routines, with a divide between the personal and the public, between family obligations and obligations to the workplace.

In theory, bureaucracies should be exemplary sites for equity. An 'ideal type' bureaucracy in a civil service avoided the favouritism and personalisation of monarchies or feudal systems – often patrimonial ones. 'Scientific' or 'classical' management theorists in North America in the early 1900s were firm advocates of bureaucratisation, attempting to make organisations run as efficiently as machines (Morgan, 1986). To achieve targets and goals, rationality and efficiency were the key, with workers selected on the basis of their ability to do a pre-determined job in the most efficient way. Nowadays, the emphasis on merit, on impersonality and on unified rules ought to mean that neither men nor women are able to gain advantage because of traditional power.

However, educational bureaucracies and the way they are now interpreted remain good sites for the play of gender power. Many are not bureaucracies in the 'ideal' sense, but use the trappings of rules and conformity in order to mask the play of power. We should ask, whose 'rationality' is in play? Whose goals take precedence? Ros Kanter, in her classic *Men and Women of the Corporation* (1977) had a strong critique of the classical rational model of bureaucracies:

> ...it focused attention on the visible, public role players, the officials with the power to 'speak for' and decide for the organisation. The focus on goals in part legitimised managerial authority on other than political grounds, for managers were conceptualised as the keepers of 'goals', while workers were seen as free to act in terms of their self interest alone... Given the concentration of women in maintenance-support functions... it was likely that the position of women and other such workers, the demands of their roles, their particularly structural situation, would be underexamined... (Kanter, 1977 op. cit. p45).

Bureaucracies, with their firm hierarchies and top-down mission statements, generate divisions between 'management' and workers. Because of new management rhetoric, in schools throughout the world we are now seeing an increase in the divide between the 'senior management team' and the mass of classroom teachers. Such a divide, as in industrial settings, may well be unbalanced in terms of gender. In addition, does the discourse of 'impartiality' prevent the flexibility which 'subordinates' may need? The acknowledgement of emotion and feeling, maternity and family leave, flexible working hours, autonomy to make decisions: all of these may be downgraded in favour of a more tightly controllable and standardised culture. Line management means having to adjust to the notions of superior-subordinate; yet our study of women and men in management mentioned earlier found some women – and men – uncomfortable with this. More collegial, rotational structures would enable less competitive people to experience management without having to leave classrooms permanently or to fragment previous relationships.

Drawn very simply, the contrasting models in practice might then be of line management and of what Ianello (1992) refers to as 'modified consensual organisation'.

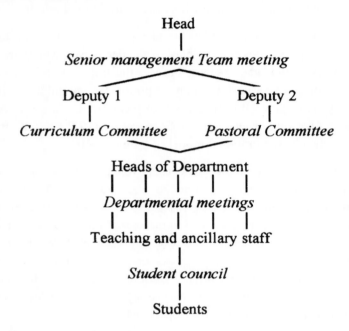

Here, in spite of the presence of committees and councils, the decision-making is predominantly linear and sited in relatively fixed positions. Things go 'up and down'. Critical decisions are made at the top; routine decisions are delegated downwards to those with information about or proximity to the decision.

In Ianello's model the organisation is represented as a circle. There is a combination of permanent elected co-ordinators and other positions which are rotational. Critical decisions are reserved for the entire membership; routine decisions are delegated horizontally to the co-ordinators. Routine decisions have the potential to become critical, in which case they can be reconsidered by the entire group. No-one works 'for' anyone else, although co-ordinators have additional authority in their areas of expertise. Clearly, this would need much unpacking in a large organisation such as a school, but it is an interesting concept which has worked well in collectives, and makes us question the inevitability of lines and pyramids.

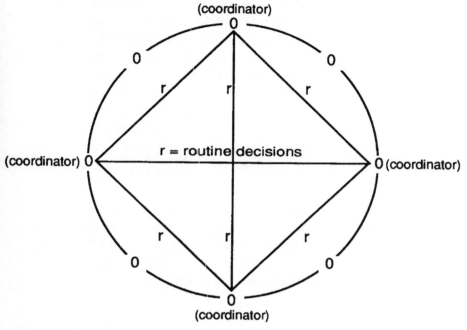

(coordinator)

(coordinator)

(coordinator)

(coordinator)

r = routine decisions

Modified Consensual Organisation

Routine decisions are made inside the circle; critical decisions are made on the circle.

Key: O – represents organisation members. Lines on the circles and within the circle represent paths of communication within the organisation.

Source: Ianello (1992) *Decisions without Hierarchy: feminist interventions in organisation theory and practice.*

There are indeed times when a strong direction is needed, particularly in times of crisis or externally driven change, and it would be foolish to say that all decisions should be democratic, consultative or participative. The point Clive Harber and I make in our (1997) book is that many apparent bureaucracies are in fact bureaucratic facades. They are hierarchical without being necessarily efficient, power is concentrated at the top without decisions being made, subordinates fear to break rules while superiors mismanage and bend the rules to their advantage. This has clear gender implications. Even apparently democratic structures within bureaucracies, such as committees, may mask the fact that the 'gatekeepers' are predominantly male. In her study of teacher education in Botswana, Mannathoko (1994) explored the flatter 'professional' bureaucracy of the University. A series of committees replaced top-down management, within apparently full participation. Yet the reality was that policies, plans and regulations had to go through the various committees and as they moved up the ladder and got cleared, they did not necessarily go back down again. The top (predominantly male) management could quite easily use the committees to delay or block implementation of policies and programmes they did not favour. This was done by arguing that new proposals were not up to standard, proper procedures had not been followed, or consultation had not been done.

Is bureaucracy then used as a cloak for authoritarianism (management by decree) and/or patriarchy (the exercise of power through the 'father' head)? Clues to the latter can also be found in thinking about how far the organisational ethos either *prevents or sustains* abuses of power such as violence (bullying or corporal punishment) and sexual harassment.

Democratic practice

What is common to authoritarianism, bureaucracy and patriarchy is *hierarchy*, the attempt to maintain dominance by subordinating others. It is based on a vertical conception of power and status – that you cannot be respected unless you are superior. Democracy, on the other hand, is based on the notion of equal respect, on the premise that it is possible to improve everyone's life situation co-operatively rather than competitively. Democracy is often seen as the antithesis to authoritarianism, and a golden ideal. Yet democracy refers not to an end state, but to a political process. The three tenets of democracy for me are *transparency, participation and challenge*, that is, a system where:

- the ways of operating are open and clear to everyone, and those in power are accountable

- there are mechanisms for people to participate in decisions on matters that affect them

- the organisation is continuously open to criticism and change through legitimised formal and informal processes of challenge, such as opposition parties or a free press.

Democracy therefore by definition carries within it the seeds of resistance and the possibilities of change.

The Overseas Development Administration[1] parameters of 'good governance' have parallels with democratic practice. The four criteria are *legitimacy, accountability, administrative competence* and *human rights* (British Council, 1993). Translated into educational terms, and with an eye on gender, we would see whether people in authority in schools or Ministries were properly appointed or elected and whether there are formal channels for open protest and alternatives to that authority (legitimacy). Secondly, we would look for proper audit procedures, to expose nepotism, corruption and abuses of power (accountability); thirdly we would want to see management with the skills to make and implement policy, to communicate it, and to distribute resources fairly (competence); and finally we would look for recognition of children's and teachers rights, in particular freedom of thought, expression, freedom to participate in decisions affecting them, and freedom from mental or physical violence (human rights).

It can be seen that democracy is not just about 'levels' of participation (as these were fairly high even in Nazi Germany) but about *how* we participate. Values of tolerance of diversity, of respect for others, and of laying decisions open to criticism might be central. Conventionally, two forms of democracy are distinguished, 'weak' and 'strong'. Weak (or representative) forms of democracy are characterised by people voting for others to represent their interests, but devolving power upwards to expertise or authority vested in that representative. Strong (or participative) forms of democracy entail participation at the appropriate level, what has been called 'statistical democracy'. This means that:

- *everyone* with a legitimate interest in a decision has a right to representation in respect of that decision and

- *only* those with a legitimate interest in a decision have a right to representation.

In school terms, this means a system of small groups, committees or 'houses' whereby all students and staff can participate, *but in forums appropriate to them.*

Both forms of democracy, weak and strong, might be in operation in an educational institution, depending on scale or size; but it is important to correct two possible misapprehensions. Firstly, democracy is not just about voting or automatic majority rule. Voting carries with it the problems of how minority views are heard, of how voters are persuaded, and of whether the issue being voted on is indeed what is important to people. In an organisation that is unbalanced in gender or ethnicity, straightforward voting – especially on an equity issue – may not ameliorate power interests. Other forms of consensual conflict resolution, mediation, channels for grievance procedures, representation and mandating are equally important. Ground rules need to be in operation about how voices are heard, who collects and interprets views and needs of members, who speaks in what arena, even who can interrupt whom.

The second point about democracy is that it is ultimately more efficient. There is an assumption that because it appears time-consuming and argumentative, it is a luxury that cannot be afforded in times of government pressure for 'reform'. Yet it is clear from many of the successful attempts at democratic schooling in developing countries (reported in Davies and Harber, 1997) that this is a road that some systems are prepared to go down in order to have schools match national goals and economic imperatives. Similarly, we report individual schools or their heads who have accepted more equitable participation by students and staff in decision-making, and examination results have actually gone up. If introduced gently, and with willingness to accept that mistakes will be made, it works.

Intervention and Training

Gender interests are best served not by having more women 'at the top' but by having structures in place which promote equity and by having people of both sexes who believe in and abide by those structures. I have argued that democratic structures are better suited to this task than are bureaucratic hierarchical ones. However, we are more used to the latter, and it is likely that systematic change will not be achieved without some intervention at the pre-service, in-service or management training level. Some initiatives target gender in particular, for example, 'women and leadership'; if this is to be done, I prefer a much broader range than just the 'skills' for leadership, and I prefer men to be targeted as well. The model outlined below has three components: auditing, micro-politics and management.

Institutional audit

It may seem strange to begin with this, but I found research to be a central activity when I was considering ways to move from authoritarian modes of organising schools (Davies, 1994). Rather than merely wanting to have more or better women in school management, we need to go back a step to establish what schools are for. If, for example, a school or country says that schools are about citizenship, about learning the skills to participate in the community, then we would expect to find evidence in those schools that students are participating in decision-making, learning political or democratic skills, and understanding issues of social structure such as ethnic or gender inequality. The reality, in my experience, is that while there is rhetoric about schooling for democracy, schools actually teach and organise in profoundly anti-democratic ways. In their Constitutions or Five-Year Plans, governments of many countries may list issues such as gender equality as priorities (Davies, 1986); yet if we examine the syllabus of their teacher training institutions, there may be little which either prepares women teachers or provides skills of gender analysis for all teachers.

Training is needed in auditing. This refers not to a degree level qualification, but simply to the habit of establishing evidence for change and continuity. There can be 'soft' and 'hard' ways of researching gender cultures in education, which complement each other well. A 'soft' way into exploring one's own workplace is what I call '*institutional anthropology*'. I have used this for in-service training as well as in staff development. Here one reflects on the discourses and styles in the organisation by means of simple sounding questions such as:

• Who does what in your organisation? What shapes would you use to draw it? Who occupies which positions? Are these permanent or rotating? What are the formal and informal networks?

• What are the 'languages' of management? What are the metaphors used when people talk about the way they organise others (militaristic? sporting? familial?) How are people referred to?

- Who are the heroes, the heroines, the villains and the fools? Why are they cast in this way? What are the legends of the organisation? What are the jokes, and the 'in-jokes', that people tell and re-tell?

- What are the rites and rituals? Who is prominent in these?

- Is this culture gendered? How does this affect you? Note instances when, in your institution, you have felt either powerless or uncomfortable or powerful or comfortable *as a woman or as a man.*

In this way, one begins to establish whether the style of the organisation lends itself to particular sorts of dominance emerging.

Performance indicators, the apparently 'harder' forms of audit, try to attach numbers to such patterns. It is conventional in education to work on indicators for effective schools, usually including such quantitative elements as examination results or attendance rates. Performance indicators for equity and democracy are harder to establish, but nonetheless are essential to goals of education in their own right and how they are (or are not) being achieved. The *Equal Opportunities* audit is now a traditional way of appraising a school or college – at least in some Western countries. Through checklists and factual data one looks at curriculum offerings, pupil take-up, pupil achievements and destinations, staffing, promotions, resources, and gender or ethnic stereotyping in textbooks. I have worked with a number of colleagues from different parts of the world to establish indicators for democratic practice in schools (Davies, 1995), which include the presence or absence of a Student Council, participation in decision-making, transparency in communication, open mechanisms for promotion and professional development, freedom of expression, whether students ask questions in class, and forums and processes for dissent and debate.

Training in 'research skills' for female – or male – leadership is not then necessarily about computer packages and multivariate analysis, more the encouragement of the facility to think sideways about what would constitute a problem and what a shift or solution. A key element in this is of course the introduction to action research. One can gain technical know-how from courses or books, but professional know-how can be gained only through attempting change in one's classroom or institution and evaluating the results. A very small shift such as changing a gendered set of tasks that students normally do, or attempting to change the gendered language of committee reports can generate a great deal of data and also raise awareness of participants. This requires some awareness of the methods and limitations of intervention, but also the confidence to engage in innovation and to enlist help or predict opposition where appropriate. The links with the micropolitics of an institution become very clear.

Micro-Politics

As implied above, many management courses do not have sustainability because they fail to deal with micropolitics of an institution or local politics. I would argue that things like time management are not technical skills but political issues, in terms of both the politics of the family and the community as well as the organisation. Leadership training for women is about turning them into political animals, and not avoiding the uncomfortable collisions that will surface. Feminist attacks on the 'glass ceiling' (Davidson and Cooper, 1992) which prevents women from reaching top positions argue that women must network, form alliances and analyse spheres of influence in the same way that men are supposed to do, for power-broking can rarely be achieved just through personal merit. In our own in-service courses at the University of Birmingham on *Personal skills for women and men in educational management*, we analyse and practise not just chairing meetings, but also the whole process of participating in them. Much successful committee work is knowledge of their mathematics (how many people it takes to 'swing' a committee if the majority appear undecided), the timing of interventions, and the preparation and follow-through for ensuring agreement and implementation of decisions. The merit of a case on the day is not necessarily enough. While I have been advocating strongly democratic forms of organisation with ultimate transparency about processes and decision-making, this does not deny that any organisation is going to have people with varied experience and skill in working within such democracies. The task in training for leadership is to alert people to the benefits of transparent democratic processes while providing skills to recognise – and challenge – any attempted circumvention of such processes.

This is particularly true for courses focusing on women, where female positioning within power complexes is crucial. Simply doing exercises on 'delegation skills' or 'time management' will remain at the exercise level unless participants are encouraged to consider who actually controls tasks and why, and how a local culture might preclude any sharpening up of one's use of the day. For example, the reasons why a headteacher does not delegate may be linked to all sorts of semi-official and even corrupt use of resources (Davies and Harber, 1997). One does not delegate use of the school grounds if one wants to graze one's own cattle on them. One does not delegate examination arrangements if one has a vested interest in selling the examination questions to the highest bidder, nor delegate budgets if one fears that a subordinate will simply pocket the proceeds. Gender cultures are particularly important here: my research on power cultures in contexts of stringency found that discourses of 'insatiable male drive' and 'female temptresses' were used to justify all sorts of illicit relationships between male teachers (or heads) and their female students (Davies, 1992). Local expectations about deference patterns and authority may complicate 'efficient' ways of sharing power.

This is where knowledge of the appropriate structures to challenge gender inequity becomes important. It is not enough for an institution to say that we would like more women in management. Appointments and promotions need clear procedures for advertising, interviewing and establishing job descriptions and requirements, so that existing senior staff do not just replicate or clone themselves. Channels for complaint or grievance have to be established, so that there are clear messages about what will and will not be tolerated. Sexual harassment – common across the world in different forms – needs an agreed and clear definition, so that people are aware of the behaviour that can be challenged under that label. Processes for consultation and participative decision-making need to be established and upheld. Minority voices require a platform and accurate recording in minutes of meetings or notes on appraisal. None of the above is restricted to democracies, and could well be simply 'imposed' by a powerful manager. Yet it is my contention that they work better if they have been argued about and agreed. A gender-sensitive organisation is also good for the bulk of men.

Disciplined democracy can avoid the worst excesses of nepotism, patriarchy and unconscious cloning. Proper job appointments prevent the nepotistic 'old boy' (or even 'old girl') network whereby relatives and friends are earmarked for posts. Job descriptions or specialisations decided not by 'superiors' but drawn up, agreed to and monitored by wide groups of interested parties, hinder the unconscious appointment or promotion of people that 'match' those already in power, those who will 'fit in'.

Management

I would argue that only when a framework of research and political awareness has been established can one move on to the technical management skills. These can be found in any management textbook: leadership styles, decision-making skills, delegation, management of time, finance and budgets. Skills are often neatly parcelled under such headings, so that 'management of resources' is seen as separate from 'management of people', when in fact both are linked to the political question of the distribution of scarce goods. Nonetheless, there is a place for basic competencies whether these are technical or professional, for example, in using spreadsheets or in approaches to appraisal.

Assertiveness training and advocacy skills could have been put under the 'political' dimension, but are placed here as they are often covered in a portfolio of personal skills that women and men managers need. As with time management, assertiveness ideologies are fraught with imperialist connotations, and are not easily translatable into different cultural contexts. That we have equal rights to state what we want may be an alien notion to some, but it is the bed-rock of transparency in relationships. Even if unsuccessful, the daring that you feel when you first say 'no' is immeasurable. If nothing else, assertiveness habits buy time – sometimes a precious commodity for women. The habit of not saying 'yes' immediately, but 'I'll think about it and let you know', is one important strategic way of reclaiming control. Questions of control at the policy level are similarly critical. The British Council is engaged in work on advocacy skills with women in many countries, particularly after the Fourth United Nations Conference for Women in Beijing in 1995 (British Council, 1996a and b). Techniques of drafting agendas, policy and resolutions, of lobbying and of persuasion, seem to me to be as appropriate to the education sphere as to the legal one.

Linked to leadership training are skills of appraisal and mentoring. Many countries are introducing more formal mechanisms for appraisal in education, whether in Ministries or in schools and colleges. However, as I have observed in Zimbabwe and Botswana, this can be seen as a judgmental activity rather than a developmental one. Appraisees are observed at work, or submit worksheets, but do not have any clear idea as to what happens to these, nor how they affect promotion. Developmental appraisal on the other hand invites appraisees to reflect on what they have achieved over the past year and what their targets might be for the coming year. The interview is to discuss that 'performance', in the light of institutional needs, and devising action plans for both appraisee and appraiser. It particularly important for women who may not go on to make demands of the system and of themselves. Earlier, I mentioned our findings that women were no less or more inclined to plan long-term careers than men. Nonetheless, women are not achieving the positions of influence in the same proportions, and the strategies to alter that imbalance include both personal career mapping and transparent institutional succession planning, so that jobs are publicly projected as far as is appropriate in uncertain times.

If we summarise all these areas under the three headings of audit, micro-politics and management, it is useful to conceive of three over-lapping circles (see opposite).

The placing may be arbitrary, but the message is that 'leadership skills' cannot be taught or learned except within a context of politically aware research, a context of an understanding of the organisation. Where the three spheres intersect is in the analysis and use of power, and it is here that change can occur. I dislike the phrase 'know your enemy' because of its militaristic connotations, and the inference in gender research that men are the enemy; yet it is important to understand at least the workings of systems, groups and individuals who may have agendas different from one's own, or from the pursuit of equity.

Equity for what?

The reason I place gender issues in management within the wider context of democracy in education is that the reasons for equity are not just rights for women themselves, but are about linking schools to wider questions of peace and national development. In educational terms, we have to think not only about whether our institutions are equitable and democratic in their own right, but about how far they prepare children for a more equitable and more democratic society. The research on the *effects* of democratic schooling internationally is scattered and sparse, as are truly democratic schools, but the indications are that children educated in a more democratic regime not only are in later life more tolerant and politically aware, but that in their school career they show higher levels of academic achievement (Harber, 1995). 'Good' education is by definition anti-sexist and anti-racist. It is not about tortoises overtaking hares, or even being 'as good as' hares. It is not about competitive races at all, particularly not between women and men. This is why I argue for policy and training which embeds gender in a holistic organisational appraisal, to strive for a democratic institution where all injustice can be brought to the surface and challenged.

Note

1. Now renamed the Department for International Development (DfID).

References

Albrow, M. (1970) *Bureaucracy*. London, Macmillan

British Council (1993) *Good Government Development Priorities: Guidelines*. Manchester: British Council.

British Council (1996a) *The Network Newsletter: Gender and Law Issue*. July 1996, No 10, Manchester: British Council.

British Council (1996b) *The Network Newsletter: Gender and Politics Issue*. November 1996, No 11, Manchester: British Council.

Brookner, A. (1984) *Hotel du Lac*. London: Jonathan Cape.

Davidson, M. and Cooper, C. (1992) *Shattering the Glass Ceiling*. London: Paul Chapman.

Davies, L. (1986) Policies on Inequality in the Third World: dependency or autonomy? In *British Journal of Sociology of Education* Vol. 7, No. 2 pp 61-75

Davies, L. (1987) Research Dilemmas Concerning Gender and the Management of Education in Third World Countries. In *Comparative Education* Vol. 23, No. 1 pp 85-94

Davies, L. (1992) School Power Cultures Under Economic Constraint. In *Educational Review*. Vol. 43, No. 2 pp 127-36

Davies, L. and Gunawardena, C. (1992) *Women and Men in International Management: the Challenge for Transparency*. Paris: IIEP

Davies, L. (1994) *Beyond Authoritarian School Management: the Challenge for Transparency*. Ticknall: Education Now.

Davies, L. (1995) 'International Indicators of Democratic Schools'. In Harber, C. (ed) *Developing Democratic Education*. Ticknell: Education Now.

Davies, L. and Harber, C. (1997) *School Management and Effectiveness in Developing Countries: the Post-bureaucratic school*. London: Cassell.

Harber, C. (1989) *Politics in African Education*. London: Macmillan.

Harber, C. (1995) 'Democratic Education and the International Agenda' in Harber, C. (ed) *Developing Democratic Education*. Ticknall: Education Now.

Ianello, K. (1992) *Decisions without hierarchy: feminist interventions in organisation theory and practice*. London: Routledge.

Kanter, R. (1977) *Men and Women of the Corporation*. New York: Basic Books.

Mac an Ghaill, M. (1994) *The Making of Men: masculinities, sexualities and schooling*. Milton Keynes: Open University Press.

Mannathoko, C. (1994) Democracy in the Management of Teacher Education in Botswana. *British Journal of Sociology of Education* Vol. 15, No. 4 p 481-495.

Morgan, G. (1986) *Images of Organisation*. Beverley Hills: Sage.

Weber, M.B. et al (1981) Why Women are Underrepresented in Educational Administration. In *Educational Leadership*. January 1981 p.320.

Chapter 3

Gender neutral leadership: a myth nurtured by leadership?

Venitha Soobrayan

In South Africa, the commitment of the African National Congress (ANC – the majority party in government) to non-sexism and non-racialism are enshrined in the constitution.[1] This means that in legal terms there is, to some extent, a levelling of the gender playing field, or should I say battlefield. However this is a very recent development; the new constitution was formally accepted only in January 1997. How effective these principles may be remains to be seen. What is apparent though is that constitutional principles of equality are not easily enforced. It would for example be difficult, were a woman to be unsuccessful in a job application, for her to prove discrimination.

Coupled with the constitutional entrenchment of equality is a strong call for a system of affirmative action to undo the damages of the past. This includes a policy for women who have generally been excluded from public and political life. This call has been premised on the belief that a simple equality of opportunity system will not be effective. Instead women activists and academics have called for a restructuring of the relations of power in organisations and institutions. The ethos, structure, functioning and policy of social and political organisations will need to change if equity is to be achieved. In an interview with women parliamentarians it became clear that the institutionalised lower status of women and the patriarchal perceptions of their inferiority endures. Frene Ginwala, the first women Speaker of Parliament had this to say:

> We are in Parliament and we are ecstatic that we have women parliamentarians and cabinet ministers here, but we will remain just parlia-

mentarians who are struggling to get women's rights on the agenda, unless we have the support and the backing of a strong South African women's movement. *Agenda*, 24, 21

This view is reinforced by Brigitte Mblandla, a woman parliamentarian:

Attitudes in Parliament are so annoying. Men parliamentarians still regard us as women in the stereotypical sense and the sad part is that they do this unconsciously. When women in parliament make a point that is important and crucial to the discussion, male parliamentarians have the ability to emphasise the correctness and relevance of the statement in a very paternalistic and patronising way. *Agenda*, 24, 21

In order to address the problems they experienced female MPs in South Africa tried to set up an inter-party women's caucus. This was met with strong opposition from male parliamentarians. It was argued (by the men) that it would compromise party political positions. The women however felt that the men were afraid of a strong women's lobby. Women could not agree with the men that calling for a creche at parliament, or drawing attention to the need for more women's toilets in the building which had previously catered mainly for men, compromised party politics.

It is increasingly clear that placing women into positions of power is not in itself a solution. These women still have many more hurdles to overcome. They have taken up positions that have previously have been held by men. For the majority of black men and women and for the majority of white women it is their first time in parliament. No males have as yet complained of the maleness of the institution; they do not seem to be aware of the maleness of the institution at all.

In calling for a women's movement to strengthen women's fight for their 'rights', Ginwala in *Agenda* (op.cit) is implicitly recognising that parliament alone is not going to do this, nor is a scattering of women in positions of power throughout the country sufficient for effective challenge of the institutionalised obstacles that confront women. There needs to be a fundamental challenge to the culture which devalues and attempts to submerge women into an all-encompassing male omnipotence.

I want to examine the concept of leadership and the implications for women. I aim to show that women are implicitly excluded from the pool of potential leaders by virtue of being women. I am applying the argument to education, for it is here that individuals, as pupils, teachers, parents or administrators, both create and act out societal expectations.

Secondly, I shall look at the experiences of women who are in leadership positions in order to demonstrate that removing the structural impediments and social prejudices that prevent women from being promoted requires recognition of the sexism inherent in the structure and practice of social and political institutions, and action which overcomes this.

The alleged (in)ability of women head teachers to maintain discipline has often been cited as a 'reason' for excluding women from leadership in schools. A popular question that endures in interview panels is whether an aspiring woman candidate for the post of headteacher is 'tough enough to discipline unruly boys'. The job is immediately gendered because it is expected that a tough man would be able to enforce discipline.

Interestingly, the women at the British Council Seminar rejected volubly the view that women are unable to enforce discipline. They all argued that they were able to exercise discipline very well. This may of course be of significance in that as all the participants at the Seminar occupied senior or very senior positions in education in their respective countries, they had demonstrated an 'unusual ability to control unruly boys.' In fact the participants admitted to using the fact that they were women to achieve discipline. One pointed out that in her culture women were mother figures in the community and it was anathema to disobey one's mother and so they could exercise discipline in this way. In my own school[2] the problem of gangsterism was very severe. Male teachers complained of finding it impossible to discipline gang members in the class. I found no such difficulty – they were very good in my class. Upon probing I discovered that these male teachers had tried to use some form of aggression to discipline them. The boys saw this as a challenge. They were 'men' competing for power. The result was that the male teachers could exercise no authority over these boys. Being male had in fact worked against them.

My first impulse in thinking about the issue of whether leadership is gendered or not, was to dismiss it with the conviction that there was in fact no debate. I thought, 'Of course leadership was gendered! Debating the issue was like debating whether the sun rises in the east or west.' Much to my surprise not everybody thought as I did. At the British Council Seminar of the twenty five participants (excluding the organisers) comprising twenty one women and four men, only one other woman and I expressed the view that leadership was indeed gendered. At the time my response to the debate was instinctive and even somewhat emotional rather than intellectually developed. The others believed that one's style of leadership rested unequivocally on personality; the characteristics of leadership were human characteristics and could not be assessed in gendered terms. Their arguments hinged mainly on their experiences as people in leadership positions and did not appear to be supported by theoretical understandings of leadership and gender. (But neither were mine!) They said that their experiences suggested that there were women and men leaders who were aggressive and authoritarian and those who were democratic and approachable; the type of leader one became had nothing to do with one's gender, and there was no particular style of leadership that could be described as being typically male or typically female.

To me this attitude seemed to be at odds with their own strongly expressed view that it was very difficult for women to attain positions of leadership; indeed many of the participants recounted their own struggles in achieving their current posts. What began to emerge was that while the majority believed that sexism against women was rife in education institutions and structures and that men sought to hold onto positions of power, the positions of power in themselves were gender neutral. The problem then was simply a mathematical one; very few women occupied positions of power despite the fact that they often were numerically superior to men at all other, that is lower, levels of education. The solution was fairly easy to determine; more women should be promoted to positions of power. The process of achieving this required struggle. The South African experience though, as described by the women parliamentarians earlier in this paper, suggests that this approach has major shortcomings.

However, my contention against the above view is that the position of leadership, irrespective of who occupies the position, is gendered. The process of reaching positions of leadership is too. The actual position of leadership and the process of getting there are not mutually exclusive. Liberal feminists may propose achieving the former without addressing the latter. The status quo of power relations in society remains intact; a few women would merely relocate to do the job previously done by a man, without really rocking the boat. It must be noted that this chapter does not face the issue of whether there are typical male and female leadership styles, although this would indeed be a matter worth investigating.[3]

It is important to recognise that the concept of leadership does not enjoy any ontological status free from the machinations of society. Prior to the development of complex social, political and economic structures, leadership may have been determined mainly through brute strength. Subsequently it might have been military acumen. 'Scholars have been able to analyse the seeds of male leadership by studying the lives of presidents and generals.' (Cantor and Bervay, 1992) An increasingly complex society meant increasingly complex demands of leadership. In other words the demands on leadership hinged on the particular historical conjuncture.

I have deliberately not attempted to define leadership for I believe that definitions are far from enduring and because definitions only acquire meaning within particular contexts. However, a common thread is that leadership has meant that certain individuals or groups of individuals are set apart from others. Also, varying degrees of power have been attributed to the position.

The fact that leaders have almost always been male is a sociological phenomenon that cannot be analysed as a sustained coincidence carried through the centuries. It seems that a prerequisite for leadership has been to be male. I am certain that it was not the having of a penis that determined leadership, although it might have been a primary qualifier for the race, but that only certain characteristics were seen to be the attributes necessary for leadership. Whatever these qualities for leadership were and even though they may have changed through the centuries, women did not have them. If one accepts the dialectical relationship between a social phenomenon and society, then the concept of leadership and the individuals that occupy positions of leadership enjoy a reciprocal relationship. It follows that since leadership has historically been occupied mainly by men, they would have had primary influence in determining its conceptual boundaries. In short men have enjoyed hegemony over the conceptualisation of leadership, and hegemony over the positions of leadership. It is widely accepted by sociologists that understandings of leadership have hinged on the male-as-norm and that women who have been leaders have been seen as exceptions to the norm. The situation still obtains today as is evidenced by the abundance of statistics on the small numbers of women in positions of authority in education institutions (Davies, 1990, Acker, 1989).

Interestingly, the woman who is usually quoted as the example that leadership is not the exclusive terrain of men, Margaret Thatcher, is often described as a woman who was not very womanly, the 'Iron Lady', the woman who entered a man's world. The challenge for women who are now beginning to achieve positions of leadership is whether to transform themselves to fit into a preconceived role or to redefine leadership in terms of their own experiences and ways of thinking. I believe that women who become leaders are increasingly taking the bold step of breaking new ground. They are challenging the stereotype of what women leaders are supposed to be, that is, like men, they are giving value to their own skills; they are giving expression to their own conceptions of leadership.

In her book: *The Female Advantage: Woman's Ways of Leadership*, Sally Helgesen interviews Dorothy Brunson, owner and president of Brunson Communications, who says that:

> the organisations in which they [women] work have for the most part been fashioned entirely 'without the ideas, brains and creative instincts of women'. (Helgesen, 1995 p229)

The title of Helgesen's book bears testimony to her belief that women's conceptions of leadership are very different from those of men. This is borne out by the four women she interviews each of whom is head of a large corporation. Each of the women suggests that her vision of leadership has definitely been shaped by the fact that she is a woman. Having to balance domestic, personal and public life is a function of being a woman. According to Helgesen:

> ...men function purely as managers, their identity seeming to exist in a vacuum untouched by the details of their personal lives.... Women do not separate their personal selves from their workplace selves; they do not split being a mother off from being a manager. (Helgesen, 1995 p67)

A common experience of many headteachers, detailed in Skelton (1989), was the struggle against the established grain in initiating their own ways of leadership. Lesley Hart writes:

> All the Heads felt that they had to win the respect of their staffs by having firm ideas of policy, but they wanted to be facilitators in a democratic process of determining policy rather than be dictators. (Hart, 1989 p103)

Because they were trying to establish a democratic process in their schools many were regarded as weak. One of the respondents interviewed says, 'I think that some people think that it's a weakness to have a democratic style of management'.

A woman head who tries to establish procedures and mechanisms that differ from her male predecessor's often encounters resistance from her staff. Miriam David describes her experience as a newly appointed headteacher:

> I did not merely want to 'add-on' a liberal feminist or woman's approach to the usual social science frame. I was inevitably different in style from the previous incumbent not just because I was a woman but also because I was an active feminist. (David, quoted in Acker, 1989 p211)

In trying to establish her own style of leadership she found that she

> quickly drew a blank in every direction [she] pursued, and ... rapidly became extremely disheartened.

She goes on to to say that she

> felt like a stranger in a foreign land, not understanding the language, habits or culture of the people of whom [she] had become a part. (Ibid, p212)

Since leadership entails varying levels of power the position is not handed out willy nilly. In reality it is hardly ever handed out at all. It is usually fought for and won. One of the fundamental premises of a patriarchal society is that power is vested in the hands of men. Public power has historically been out of the reach of women. It can be argued that women should now enter the battlefield and do battle if they want to attain positions of leadership. The problem of course is that the rules of war have already been set and from where do they get the necessary ammunition to enter the battle? If women are to achieve positions of leadership, in other words if they are to lay claim to a level of social power, then they would have to challenge the tenets of patriarchy. As far as leadership goes this would mean defining for themselves what leadership means and offering their own ways of leading and managing as being valuable and authentic. They should not find themselves being prescribed to and proscribed by a male leadership tradition.

Discourses of leadership also exclude women. In the first instance the sexual imagery used to describe success immediately renders women impotent; for example one needs 'balls' to get to the top. The word serves not only as a crude description of male genitals but it simultaneously describes a personality attribute. Since women are physiologically excluded from the having of 'balls', the implication is that they are excluded from the supposedly equivalent characteristics of courage and guts and confidence. 'Getting to the top' and 'screwing' the opposition are also sexual images of power that are not usually part of female sexual discourse. One may argue that this is an outdated and conservative position that ignores the sexual liberation of today. Movies of the *Basic Instinct* genre may suggest a sexual emancipation that renders my opinion outdated. But the success of such movies rests on the very point I am making; they are different from the norm, they challenge the stereotype, but do not necessarily change it. The same holds true for the comic success of a movie like *Kindergarten Cop* where a large, swarthy but clumsy man is put into a role usually occupied by a woman.

Of course the most versatile word that transcends all cultures, languages, situations and gender, is 'fuck'. In the corporate world it eloquently describes one's attitude to the opposition; it is a winning attitude that inspires success. Of course one has to have 'balls' in order to 'fuck' the opposition. As shown above, whether one chooses to read this literally or metaphorically, women are excluded from its parameters. Interestingly, the same word, with the appropriate intonation, is used to describe a man's sexual conquering of a woman. Perhaps the thrill of male power here echoes the satisfaction of conquering the opposition, thereby strengthening the notion of power and leadership being the domain of men?

Sports metaphors of being 'part of the team', of 'playing the game', of 'playing by the rules' of competitiveness and winning are other discourses of power that abound within the corporate hierarchy. According to Helgesen women who have reached senior levels in corporate institutions have been urged to learn the game of football.

> Football was assumed to parallel business in a number of specific ways: its organisational structure, its tenacious focus on objective, its obsession with blocking the competition, its emphasis on the deployment of efficient units, and its need for team players who do what they're told and do not question the coach. (Helgeson, 1995 op.cit. p36)

Such an orientation signals an inflexible hierarchy that survives on the strict preservation of rules. If the overwhelming majority of women have not been imbued with the culture of football they become automatically excluded from the culture of leadership as well. In her study of female psychology Carol Gilligan observes:

> Male children learn to put winning ahead of personal relationships or growth; to feel comfortable with rule, boundaries, and procedures; and to submerge their individuality for the greater goal of the game. Females learn to value cooperation and relationships; to disdain complex rules and authoritarian structures; and to disregard abstract notions like the quest for victory if they threaten the harmony of the group as a whole. (Gilligan in Helgeson, p38, ibid)

It may be argued that this is a simplistic generalisation that does not hold true for all children. However the validity of her research is not the issue. The point is that this perception has historically been implemented in the process of selecting leadership. It is this alleged quality that has rendered women incompatible with the demands of leadership. It is a conviction commandeered by those in power to present women as not being authoritative enough, being too concerned with emotions and not having a strong will to win. While it may be that women might not have the qualities described above, Helgesen says that this is not an impediment but an advantage.

> As historical outsiders to such [leadership] positions, women often had fresh eyes to see what was no longer working and to identify new solutions. In addition, women were bringing into the workplace talents that had for years been considered of value only in the private, domestic sphere. (Helgesen, 1995:xiv).

A study of the experiences of women managers suggests that they have different conceptions of what constitutes good leadership skills. A textbook (Calitz et al, 1992) on school management used at the teacher training college where I am employed promotes leadership styles that many women leaders would find unacceptable. In addition to the gross practice of using the male pronoun throughout the text and thereby implicitly and explicitly excluding women from the parameters of leadership, the text makes some very trite recommendations that are reminiscent of archaic understandings of education and of leadership. For example the text in question suggests that interaction with people in the school must be kept to an 'absolute minimum' in order to use time efficiently, that administrative time is wasted because conversations are 'not brief and to the point' and that principals should be able to 'use' their secretaries more 'effectively' (Calitz op.cit. p23).

On the other hand the women leaders interviewed by Helgesen all felt that relating to people within their organisations was of primary importance, working *with* people and sharing ideas was preferred to using people; establishing a non-hierarchical system that was inclusive in its culture was seen as preferable to rigid top-down hierarchies, and that making time for unscheduled meetings and people's needs was of extreme importance to the harmony of their institution. The women leaders in Ozga's *Women in Educational Management* (1993) express similar opinions.

I am aware that it is very difficult to 'prove' that there are typical male and female characteristics. Some feminists may even argue that it is anathema to feminism to distinguish male and female characteristics as this would only serve to undermine women even further and to reinforce prescriptive stereotypes. Lynn Davies suggests that it would be more constructive to move away from emphasising differences and seek commonalities that would foster a non-sexist society through democracy. Clearly the majority of the participants at the British Council Seminar did not think there are typical male and female characteristics; instead there is simply a large pool of characteristics that men and women could choose from as they wished. To extrapolate this view, the kind of leaders men and women become is dependent entirely on the personality choices they make.

It would be short-sighted to think that we make choices, if we make them at all, as free agents. Suggesting that who we are is simply a matter of conscious decision neutralises the process of socialisation. There are also numerous social factors that influence our choices, peer pressure being one obvious and potent factor. Clearly the scope of this paper does not allow for a full discussion of personality determinants. I am not certain that there are clearly defined male and female characteristics but I do believe that the process of developing character is gendered. No matter what your personality may be, being male or female is not exclusive of such personality; it is an integral part of who you are. At the one level it is bizarre to think that we grow up without ever noticing our genitals and becoming aware, in the first instance, of sex differences. While I do not equate biological sex with gender they are not mutually exclusive: gendering is rooted in biological sex.

Finally, it was agreed at the seminar that it is possible for women leaders to be aggressive as it is for male leaders to be gentle and non-aggressive. Choosing to associate aggression with the female and not with the male implies that 'aggression' and 'male' is the norm whereas 'aggression' and 'female' challenges the norm. While this reasoning hinges on the existence of stereotypes, it also reinforces my earlier point that character is unavoidably a function of gender. The quality of non-aggression is not the focus of concern; it is being male and non-aggressive that lies at the heart of the matter.

To suggest that leadership is gender neutral and simply a function of personality is to collude with a myth, for structural constraints affect, and can even prevent, the expression of personality. People who emphasise democratic process and consultation may find themselves severely constrained in a strictly hierarchical non-consultative organisation. Women participants at the seminar pointed to how their culture impinged on their effectiveness as leaders; men would not take direction from them because it was culturally unacceptable for a man to heed the word of a woman. As a leader a woman cannot respond to this difficulty in a gender neutral way since being a woman is the very essence of the problem.

Conclusion

I am left with the uneasy feeling that those in leadership may be reluctant to admit to the gendered nature of the job because it may be indicative of weakness. Having struggled through the ranks, finally getting to the top, it would be onerous to think that one's functioning in this hard-earned position is shaped by the condition of being a man or a woman. It would be far more comfortable to visualise oneself doing the job simply as a competent person. It is almost as if recognition of being a male or female in the way one functions is an admission of incompetence. Perhaps this is in itself evidence of gendering. For a woman to admit to having a woman's consciousness and not a man's would be tacit acknowledgment of being 'lesser'. A man's reluctance to admit to the gendering of the job allows him to find comfort in the belief that he enjoyed no privileges in getting the job, that is, being a man was not really a factor in his favour, that he got the job purely on the basis of merit and competence. Of course 'merit' and 'competence' are also gendered phenomena but that is material for another paper.

The illusion of gender-neutral management may be premised on out-dated management theories that stressed the need for objectivity and separation of leader from followers. Modern management theories are moving away from the leader-as-apart model and towards an understanding of leadership that encourages the cohesive wholeness of an institution and draws the various components of the institution closer together in a kind of web-like structure. However, for structural changes to be fully inclusive they have to be underpinned by a consciousness of the relationships between gendering and structure and between gendering and style of work.

While I have tried to demonstrate the unfair advantage that men enjoy by virtue of the male gendering of positions of leadership, I am not suggesting that men should not be leaders, or that they are not good leaders. Nor do I mean to imply that women would perhaps make better leaders than men. Instead, my project has been to argue for the recognition of gendering in the conceptualising of leadership and the deleterious effect this has on potential women leaders. In doing so I do not propose that we strive to make the position of leader gender neutral, but rather to attack the dogmas that circumscribe leadership, thereby rendering it immutably and exclusively gendered as male.

Acknowledgements

I would like to thank the Seminar organisers for providing the space for stimulating and enjoyable debate.

My deepest gratitude goes to the other participants who provided new insights on a variety of issues and whose views I have frequently referred to in this paper. The comments and discussion raised by them provided a starting point for my own thoughts and arguments raised here.

Notes

1. The ANC's policy is that women should make up at least 33 per cent of parliamentarians. This policy was put into effect after the first democratic elections in the country in 1994.

2. The school I refer to is a South African school that used to have a mainly 'Indian' population. In 1990 this began to change and it currently has a mix of races. The example quoted is not characteristic of any particular race. The incident referred to happened in 1992. I am no longer at this school but I was given to understand by present members of staff that a similar situation still prevails. In a recent incident (1996) a male teacher who showed aggression and tried to discipline the boys by being 'tough' had his classroom trashed and his car damaged. Other male teachers have had similar experiences. To date there have been no reports of similar behaviour towards female staff.

3. *Editors' note*: it is — see Jeanette Morris' chapter in this volume: *Good education management: women's experiences.*

References

Acker, S. (ed) (1989) *Teachers, Gender and Careers.* New York: The Falmer Press.

Acker, S. (1994) Gendered Education: Sociological Reflections on Women, Teaching and Feminism. Buckingham: Open University Press.

Agenda, (24), 21-26.

Calitz, L; Viljoen, J; Moller, T and van der Bank, A. (1992) *School Management.* Pretoria: Via Afrika Limited.

Cantor, D.W. and Bernay, T. (1992) *Women in Power: The Secrets of Leadership.* Boston: Houghton Mifflin Company.

Davies, L. (1990) *Equity and Efficiency? School Management in an International Context.* London: The Falmer Press.

David, M.E. *Prima Donna inter Pares? Women in Academic Management.* In Acker, S. (ed) (1989) *Teachers, Gender and Careers.* New York: Falmer.

Hart, L. 'Women in Primary Management'. In Skelton, C. (ed) (1989) *Whatever Happens to Little Women: Gender and Primary Schooling.* Milton Keynes: Open University Press.

Helgesen, S. (1995) *The Female Advantage: Women's Ways of Leadership.* New York: Doubleday.

Ozga, J. (ed) (1993) *Women in Educational Management.* Buckingham: Open University Press.

Skelton, C. (ed) (1989) *Whatever Happens to Little Women? Gender and Primary Schooling.* Milton Keynes: Open University Press.

Section Two
Schooling and Work

Chapters by Fiona Leach and by Zeeshan H. Rahman reveal the connections between educating girls to become women, the realities of life as women use the education they have experienced, and the gender-sensitivity of organisations which appear to prioritise education for girls and women.

Fiona Leach has written *Gender on the aid agenda: men, women and educational opportunity* from an analytical standpoint. She argues that whilst there is plenty of emphasis by donor agencies on access to basic education for girls and very basic skills training for women in developing countries, this is not supported by provision of opportunities for women to obtain complete economic independence, nor is it considered important that they should. Furthermore, education for women and girls is promoted on the grounds that it brings benefit to other people rather than themselves. Donors, Fiona Leach notes, do not promote basic education for poor women in developing countries on the grounds that education is potentially liberating for the recipients themselves, and she describes the various effects of this approach.

The strategies and structures of the donor agencies and other providers of education are shown to be inherently sexist and based on sexist assumptions about women. We see how values which are attributable to white male middle class views of the world permeate through to developing countries. Changes in the parameters of funding allocation for education provision in developing countries are also seen to work against women's interest; greater community involvement; decentralised control as well as more privatisation and cost-sharing can also be generally detrimental to the advancement of girls' education.

Zeeshan H. Rahman works for the Bangladesh Rural Advancement Committee (BRAC), the biggest non-governmental organisation in the world. BRAC has focused attention on basic education at primary level for girls since

1985, reflecting international tendencies throughout the developing world to prioritise this. Her chapter *Non-formal primary education: a gender-based programme* describes how the provision of basic education at primary level to women and girls in rural Bangladesh has generated issues of gender awareness which BRAC has had to acknowledge and discuss and to address quite specifically at all levels in the organisation. Zeeshan H. Rahman shows how the specific features of Bangladeshi rural society have driven these changes, for without women teachers and field workers prepared to go out to the people that they are trying to work with, rural girls and women will not co-operate with the education programmes. Because of this outreach the programmes have become immensely popular. The primary education programme has done a good job in providing educational opportunities, especially for young women; and because it is so popular it gives women employees some power to press for improved conditions of service. This progress continues.

Nevertheless, despite the optimistic account of activities in BRAC to promote gender sensitivity within the organisation and among BRAC's fieldworkers in the rural areas, the case study does illustrate some of the issues raised in Fiona Leach's analysis. For example, even though 1.8 million people in Bangladesh were able to save the equivalent of (collectively) one million Taka (about US$30 million) for productive projects, and even though 90 per cent were women, virtually all the women were involved in poultry projects. In other words, despite demonstrating excellent husbandry, the women were not involved in projects with high economic yield. BRAC is making progress, yet only 23 per cent of the staff are female; a proportion which is increasing, it is true, but still vastly disproportionate to the numbers of women on the receiving end of help from this NGO. BRAC's female employees have had to work hard for acknowledgement of how their workplace needs differ from those of male staff. Management is still clearly gendered to the extent that whilst 'women's issues' are considered sympathetically, women working in the organisation still have to wait for 'permission' from male superiors to implement changes.

Even though they were written independently, on opposite sides of the earth, these two chapters complement each other and merit being considered together.

Chapter 4

Gender on the aid agenda: men, women and educational opportunity

Fiona Leach

Introduction

The goal of gender equity in education has been on the agenda of national governments and international development agencies for several decades. Since the United Nations Conference in Nairobi in 1985 marking the end of the United Nations Decade for Women, it has become, along with poverty alleviation, the highest donor priority. *The World Conference on Education for All*, held in Jomtien, Thailand in 1990 added impetus because it drew attention to the fact that the major constraint on universal primary education was the low level of girls' enrolments in many parts of the world. Article 3 of the World Declaration on Education For All states that:

> The most urgent priority is to ensure access to, and to improve the quality of, education for girls and women, and to remove every obstacle that hampers their active participation. All gender stereotyping in education should be eliminated. (World Conference on Education For All (WCEFA), 1990)

The consequence of the low level of participation of women in education worldwide is clearly seen when one examines global literacy rates. It is estimated that of the 885 million illiterate adults (aged over 15 years) in the world today, approximately 70 per cent are women, and these women are likely to be amongst the very poorest. Nor is the situation improving with the younger generation; of the estimated 110 million illiterate school children aged 6-11 years, two-thirds are girls (UNESCO, 1996). Low educational levels among girls are also reflected in the under-representation of women in high-skill and professional employment and in political representation, as well as (until very recently) in the neglect of consideration of women's needs and circumstances in the design of development policy and strategy.

In Amman, Jordan in June 1996 a Mid-Decade meeting to review progress was held with those national governments and aid agencies which had committed themselves to the Education for All initiative at Jomtien. At that meeting, it became clear that of all the goals set at Jomtien, reducing the gender gap in education had met with the least success. Only a tiny percentage rise was recorded in girls' primary enrolments in developing countries comparative to boys (from 45.4 per cent of total enrolments in 1990 to 45.8 per cent in 1995 (UNESCO, 1996 op.cit). Given the extensive rhetoric around this issue internationally and specific commitments made by many governments to promote women's education, this finding is very disappointing, although not surprising. Most alarmingly, it was found that the gender gap in literacy levels worldwide had increased since 1990, as had the gap between female and male primary enrolment rates in some areas of sub-Saharan Africa and East and South Asia.

Donor support for the education of women and girls
This chapter argues that aid agencies, and the governments to whom they frequently offer advice on policy, have concentrated on increasing girls' access to education, whether through formal or non-formal channels, without paying sufficient attention to the content and its impact on women's social, political and economic status in society. In other words, aid agencies are neglecting to examine whether education is actually transforming widespread attitudes and practices in society which prevent the equality of women and men in all spheres of life, including attitudes *in the educational system itself*. Education has served largely to maintain the *status quo* in gender relations, reflecting continuing inequalities in male and female access to power and resources in the wider society, and perpetuating stereotypical male and female roles (Deem, 1980). Attempts to increase girls' enrolments worldwide have therefore taken place in a context where men usually dominate in all

areas of decision-making and authority as well as in the labour market. The benefits to the family of educating girls on equal terms with boys are not always convincing enough for a significant change of attitude to take place and for the necessary financial sacrifices to be made to place or to keep girls in school. Only eleven per cent of parliamentary seats worldwide are held by women and only ten heads of state were women in 1994 (United Nations, 1995). Figures on women managers are also not impressive, either in the developed or the developing world, e.g. in Britain in 1994 only 32 per cent of managerial/administrative positions were held by women but 76 per cent of clerical and secretarial jobs (British Broadcasting Corporation, 1994). At the executive level, in the USA in 1993 only one per cent of chief executive officers in the largest corporations were women; outside the USA none were (United Nations, 1995). In Britain, according to the British Institute of Management in 1992, three per cent of senior managers were women; in education the figures are similar (Ouston, 1993).

By failing to ensure that schooling acts as a catalyst for social change on gender issues, the development agencies, both official and non-governmental, have themselves subscribed to a narrow view of the purpose of educating women. They have promoted projects which have tended to reinforce stereotypical attitudes about appropriate gender roles, rather than projects which could help to transform society's understanding of women's past and current contribution to social and economic development as well as their unrecognised roles as leaders, managers and innovators. It has been left largely to grassroots organisations and a few international non-governmental organisations (NGOs) to engage in education projects of a transforming nature. Indeed, the agencies' approach to the education of women has reflected their approach to development which for far too long saw women as passive beneficiaries of projects and programmes designed largely by men, rather than as initiators and key players in the development process. Progress has been made in the sense that women are no longer 'invisible' on the development agenda and their particular needs are being considered through, for example, the creation of 'Women in Development' offices within the agencies, the increasing use of gender impact assessments and monitoring on projects and programmes, and gender training of agency staff (Stromquist, 1994). Despite this, women are still not given sufficient power and voice to determine their own priorities and strategies, nor are they usually given a prominent role in the planning and management of projects.

The impact of agency interventions in education on women's status

It is argued here that aid agencies have served to perpetuate unequal gender relations through their interventions in education. This argument is developed along four dimensions of analysis. These are: the *rationale* provided by donors for prioritising the education of women and girls, the *types of intervention* pursued by donors to improve women's participation in education, the *types of education and training* that donors have chosen to support over the past few decades (both formal and non-formal), and the strategies currently advocated by donors to expand educational provision for both boys and girls. In addition, viewing women as leaders and innovators in both education and development is shown to be hampered by the agencies' failure to view their own female staff in these terms and to promote them to senior positions within the organisation. Thus, the aid agencies' own gender-biased structures act as a brake on the development of aid programmes which prepare and promote women for positions of responsibility and authority, whether in community development, politics, business or public administration; and development policy and strategy regarding women continues to be made largely by men.

Rationale

With regard to the agencies' rationale for supporting the education of women and girls, these have until very recently reflected a long-standing preoccupation with child-rearing and homemaking. This is clearly seen in World Bank publications on this subject and in the type of research that the Bank sponsors[1]. It is important to note that the World Bank is now the major provider of external funds to education, committing approximately $2 billion per annum currently (having funded education only minimally until the mid 1980s) (World Bank, 1995a). The first major World Bank publication on women's education, *Women's Education in Developing Countries* (King and Hill, 1993), cites many examples of research studies where the claims of the benefits of educating women are viewed almost exclusively in terms of traditional female domestic and childrearing roles. The authors detail these benefits as follows:

> A better-educated mother has fewer and better-educated children. She is more productive at home and in the workplace. And she raises a healthier family, since she can better apply improved hygiene and nutritional practices. Education can even substitute for community health programs by informing women about health care and personal hygiene, and it can complement such programs by raising income and promoting greater recognition of the value of these services. [......] So important is the influence of mothers' education on children's health and nutritional status that it reduces mortality rates. (King and Hill op.cit. pp12-13)

Even the importance of a woman's education for her productive, as opposed to her reproductive, role is couched not in terms of her ability to earn an independent income or to contribute directly to the national economy but in terms of her contribution to family welfare:

> ..women's education also indirectly improves infant survival rates by leading to higher market productivity for women, and thus to better living standards for the family. (Ibid p18)

Where the importance of women's productive role is given due recognition, the aid literature argues for the promotion of their education on the grounds of 'improved efficiency' and 'investment in human capital'. According to this argument, the economic productivity of women is currently very low in the majority of countries and this is a wasteful use of the human potential of roughly half the adult population. If educating women can produce economic gains by enhancing their productivity as well as providing the social benefits detailed above, all the better. Stromquist in her 1994 study for UNICEF *Gender and Basic Education in International Development Cooperation* sums up the World Bank approach as continuing 'to see the treatment of gender issues as justified primarily by increased efficiency, national productivity and increased returns' (Stromquist, op.cit. p27).

The rationale for educating women to higher levels than is currently the case in most developing countries is therefore couched in terms of the social and economic gains to the family and to society, rather than in terms of the gains to women themselves. Women are treated as a commodity to be used more efficiently rather than as citizens for whom social justice is a question of principle. Education is a basic human right to be provided for women as for men and as an opportunity for women to gain greater control over their lives, in running a business, owning property, in full-time employment, or exercising their right to vote and the right to defend themselves against violence. This is seen as less important than the need for a more efficient use of human resources by the state. Consequently, donors have largely failed to remove the basic causes of women's inferior status and to see that the goal of gender equity in education cannot be achieved and women's potential maximised, either socially or economically, until the prevailing images of men and women in the wider society are transformed. If education is to be a force for change in gender relations, as is claimed by liberal feminists (Acker, 1987), then change has to come first from within the schooling process.

Types of educational intervention

There has been an excessive preoccupation with increasing access and reducing dropout and repetition rates for girls, e.g. through increasing school places, building more schools so that girls have shorter distances to travel, recruiting more female teachers, providing scholarships and free uniforms for girls, and designing flexible school schedules to accommodate girls' required labour contribution for the family (e.g. King and Hill: Chapter 8, in Tietjen, 1991). Qualitative improvements have been seen in terms of increasing the supply of textbooks and other teaching and learning materials and providing better equipped schools, smaller classes and more or better trained teachers. Changes to the process of education, in particular through revision of curriculum content to remove gender bias and promote more positive images of women and girls and gender sensitive teacher training have, as Stromquist (op.cit) points out, been crucially ignored. Issues relating to the internal functioning of the school, and in particular the influence that school processes and practices play on girls' expectations and attitudes (through both the formal and informal curriculum), have been neglected in favour of factors external to the schooling process. The role of teachers in the socialisation process, revealing all too often discouraging, dismissive and otherwise negative attitudes to girls' education, is very significant. Sadly, female teachers have on the whole been as much party to the reproduction of negative educational images of girls as their male counterparts.

Although donors have expressed concern over low academic achievement among girls in many countries, they have been slow to acknowledge the links between this low achievement and the low aspirations and low status of women in society. Indeed they have tended to refute the suggestion that teachers' attitudes towards female students or gender bias in textbooks has had any impact on girls' achievement or attendance. This is evident in King and Hill's 1993 book for the World Bank and in Tjietjen's 1991 study for USAID. Both suggest that the funds needed for eliminating bias from textbooks would be better spent on producing more textbooks and instructional materials and that 'improving the overall quality of education may be the most productive investment for attracting girls to school and keeping them there' (King and Hill, 1993, p 311). It is only in the more recent World Bank Technical Paper by Odaga and Heneveld (1995) entitled *Girls and Schools in Sub-Saharan Africa* that recognition is given to the importance of gender bias in schools.

Yet, there are a number of highly revealing small scale studies from developing countries which indicate that teacher and parental attitudes towards girls' education and the way the schooling process is organised and delivered sends subtle but powerful messages to girls about what they should expect in adult life (e.g. Gordon, 1995 on Zimbabwe, Davison and Kanyuka, 1992 on Malawi, and Duncan, 1989 on Botswana). Female students in Africa, for instance, may be expected to come early to school to clean out classrooms and to help prepare school meals. In particular, these messages underscore the authority and superiority of males and implicitly endorse gender-differentiated roles which reinforce girls' negative self-perceptions and limit their expectations.

Types of education and training

Increasing numbers of women are forced by economic hardship and deprivation to earn a living, often as sole bread-winner of the family. An estimated one-third of global households are now headed by females, and women are often the sole decision-makers both in the family and outside, being responsible for feeding the family and meeting community obligations. However, women do not compete for jobs on equal terms with men, for in most countries they enter the labour market with a lower level of skills, qualifications and experience. Where women are becoming better qualified and constitute almost 50 per cent of the labour force (as in many Western nations), they are still not promoted to positions as supervisors or managers. Employers generally perceive women to be a poor investment (they may leave to get married or have children, or they may demand maternity leave). They fail to recognise the considerable organisational and management skills acquired by women through running a household and engaging in community affairs, which provide experience and practice for positions of responsibility in the workplace. It is all the more important, therefore, to examine the extent to which aid agencies have supported the expansion of education and training opportunities for women that will help them to counteract discrimination in the labour market and enhance their prospects of securing high-skill jobs. Unfortunately, the record is not good.

Donors may have belatedly begun to acknowledge that women are heavily engaged in economic production, but they have not yet recognised that women are in need of 'real jobs' as opposed to merely moving in and out of the labour market as their circumstances dictate, earning additional income as 'pocket money' for themselves or as a supplement to the male income of the family. It is interesting in this context that the image portrayed through the media, and most importantly through school textbooks, of women fulfilling largely domestic and child-rearing roles belies the reality of most women's lives (Leach, 1996).

It is this need for women to engage in productive work which makes the type of education and training opportunity made available to women an important issue of gender equity. Girls have been traditionally discouraged from, or have tended to shy away from, studying the high status subjects of mathematics and science, which are seen as domains where boys excel (Duncan, 1989, Harding, 1992) besides being subjects which provide a passport to higher education and to professional occupations. The school curriculum as well as teachers' attitudes and informal school practices have tended to project a future for girls exclusively linked to marriage and motherhood, but for boys to waged employment, with the result that fewer girls stay on in education (in some African countries only one in four university students are female). Interestingly, even where women are well represented at the higher levels of education (e.g. in many Latin American and Caribbean countries, Botswana, Lesotho, Namibia and the Philippines), they remain seriously under-represented in skilled and particularly managerial jobs, showing that education has resulted in little transfer of economic power from men to women. Schools have to be judged, therefore, as having largely failed to treat boys and girls equally. They neither encourage both sexes to do well academically, nor do they encourage the view that education is preparation for a job or a career.

The tendency to separate girls from jobs and careers is clearly seen at the secondary level where the curriculum often offers vocational options. During the 1970s and early 1980s the development agencies, led by the World Bank, gave enthusiastic support to initiatives to make education more practical and more relevant to the needs of young people in developing countries. In these countries, skilled labour for the anticipated acceleration of economic growth was desperately needed, and vocationalising the secondary school curriculum was one way of preparing for this. This trend did not increase life opportunities for women or reduce differentiation along gender lines, for girls tended either to be denied access to training in traditional male areas or chose to avoid such subjects and to opt for courses in home economics, secretarial studies, tailoring, hairdressing and beauty-care, where jobs are usually poorly paid and which do little to strengthen women's position.

Likewise, women have always been under-represented in vocational institutes, and where they are present they are grouped in the traditional female areas. For example, in Ghana in 1992 only 9.7 per cent of total enrolments in secondary vocational and technical institutes were female (Boeh-Ocansey, 1995); in Tanzania only 20.7 per cent of trainees in The National Vocational Training Division programme were female in 1989, despite the existence of a quota system (Mbilinyi and Mbughuni, 1991), and an International Labour Organisation (ILO) study of African Polytechnics in the late 1980s (ILO, 1992) showed that only 25 per cent or less of total enrolments were female and a tiny proportion of these were on technical courses (Goodale, 1989). Even where quota systems are introduced as in the Caribbean (Ellis, 1990), peer group pressure and the fear of harassment and ridicule prevented girls from making non-traditional choices. While the situation may have improved since these data were gathered, it is clear that donor policy on vocational education has tended to reinforce gender stereotypes in education.

Much entrepreneurship training is provided through non-formal educa-tion although a few countries, most notably Kenya and Malaysia, teach business education as a subject at the end of primary school. Among governments and donors, there is a belated recognition in the poorest countries of the world that the formal labour market will not grow at the rates anticipated in the 1960s and 1970s and that most young people will need to seek work in the so-called 'informal sector' or 'shadow economy', this being in many countries a much larger source of employ-ment than the regulated formal or modern sector of the economy; (in some countries the formal sector provides as little as 10 per cent of total employment). Women are to be found in large numbers in the informal sector, often outnumbering men. They are to be found in petty trading and street vending, paid domestic labour and on construction sites and plantations. Women are easy prey to unscrupulous money-lenders and contractors and are often obliged to resort to illicit economic activity such as brewing alcohol and prostitution which makes them even more vulnerable to persecution and harassment. King (1993) describes a continuum from entrepreneurship self-employment (successful) to sub-sistence self-employment (mere survival); women are overwhelmingly to be found at the subsistence end of this continuum.

The manifest failure of initiatives in vocational education and the increasingly mobile nature of the global workforce have led donors away from supporting school-based vocational education and towards advocating a broad-based general education providing flexible basic skills, in the belief that work-related skills are best taught 'on the job' in existing enterprises. An undifferentiated curriculum should in prin-ciple be beneficial to women, especially as they appear to excel in interpersonal and communication skills which are much valued in the labour market nowadays. However, attitudes towards appropriate skills for men and women remain largely unchanged. This is evident in the development agencies' current interest in 'enterprise education' or 'education for entrepreneurship', which emphasises education as preparing young people for self-employment in particular through the acquisition of basic business and accountancy skills, either in schools (e.g. at the primary level in Kenya) or vocational training institutes or through NGO training programmes.

Women have a strong presence in small-scale self-employment and they can be highly entrepreneurial when seeking to survive economically (Appleton, 1995, Anand, 1992). Despite this, entrepreneurship education, like vocational education and training, is largely seen as a masculine area. Donor initiatives in this field couch entrepreneurship and small enterprise development in economic terms and there is a strong bias towards private sector training in relatively high status skills e.g. technology and computers, industrial design, export manufacturing etc. – all areas dominated by men. This offers stark contrast with the donor discourse and activity surrounding training initiatives with women. Here, the language and conceptual frameworks derive not from economics but from the social sciences and in a context characterised by poverty, marginalisation and community welfare. Women-only income generating projects are usually set up with a view to providing women with skills for survival, not profit, and in a setting lacking a concept of a formal enterprise with structures, physical premises, balance sheets and short and medium term plans. While the focus on poverty alleviation is justified, there is also a need to promote women as successful in business and to offer role models to young children in school of what women can achieve. The fact that women are now being increasingly recognised as more reliable recipients of credit than men may well be a first step towards supporting women more actively in business and commercial ventures.

Income generating projects for women are usually supported by non-governmental organisations. While NGOs have played a major role in reaching poor and disadvantaged people with nonformal education programmes, they are also guilty of perpetuating gender stereotypes by confining their training largely to traditional female occupations such as food production, craftwork and tailoring, which are rarely sustainable and profitable activities (not surprisingly the record of such projects in generating income is very poor; Buvinic, 1986, Goodale, 1989), and by viewing these activities as secondary to women's household duties. Ironically, but perhaps not surprisingly, those initiatives which can be viewed as ones where women play a strong leadership and decision-making role usually take the form of grassroots projects initiated by women themselves without outside support.

NGOs also support programmes of community development which provide literacy classes, basic education, health and population education for women, but all too often these have continued to reflect the same gender biases that prevail in formal education by reinforcing women's traditional domestic and child-rearing roles. For example, basic literacy for women has usually been seen as enhancing their roles as mothers and housewives, with literacy classes focusing on health, nutrition, and community development rather than on economic activities. Rogers (1994) found that even when literacy is part of a broader programme which includes income generation, the two sets of activities are kept separate so that learners are not being encouraged to use their literacy skills practically to advance their economic activities and to increase their control over their own affairs. For example the vocabulary of primers does not cover words used in economic activities, women are not encouraged to write down their financial transactions but merely to memorise them, and often the accounts of credit groups are kept by a literacy instructor or a NGO official and not by the women themselves[2].

Donor strategies

The strategies employed by development agencies to expand educational provision have not always favoured girls. Stromquist (1994) points out that while 'parents and other community members subscribe to views of girls merely as potential mothers and consider as a 'relevant' curriculum only one that trains women for domestic roles' (Stromquist op.cit. p26), the current emphasis on increasing and legitimating community control over the funding and provision of education will not serve the aim of increasing girls' participation in a wider range of curriculum activities. The same can be said of promoting church or mosque based education because these institutions do not usually espouse a broad view of women's role in society.

Likewise, the current donor ideology of increased privatisation and of cost-sharing through the introduction of school fees, usually at the secondary level but in some countries (e.g. Uganda) also at the primary level, is likely in the long run to preclude a more equitable participation of women in education. Parents who in the past did not see any clear benefit of girls' education but allowed their daughters to attend school as it was free are less likely to continue to do so if they have to pay fees or other contributions. These are increasing as governments reduce their level of funding. Current donor preference for private rather than public provision of work-related training, either 'on the job' by employers or in private training organisations (World Bank, 1991), is also likely to be detrimental to women economically because women are under-represented in formal employment where most 'on the job' training takes place, and are particularly under-represented in those occupational grades where training and skill upgrading is directed e.g. in managerial and supervisory positions. (Women are of course well represented on the assembly line, particularly in the electronics industry, where pay is low and promotion prospects few). Women also have less disposable income than men and are less likely to be able to pay for training. Policy on training for employment, therefore, continues to ignore the disadvantageous position of women in the labour market. It is significant that the World Bank policy paper on *Vocational and Technical Education and Training* (1991) devotes less than a page to women and employment and to the need to eliminate gender biases in the labour market. While attitudes are changing and women are gradually taking a more equitable share of the better paid skilled jobs, in most developing countries progress is very slow.

Decentralised control of education, as complementing privatisation and increased community involvement, is another donor strategy which may have an adverse impact on gender equity in education, for in poorer, predominantly rural, regions where available public funds are less than elsewhere and families are usually very conservative, girls' education is unlikely to be a priority.

Gender equity within the aid agencies

Finally it should be noted that the international agencies themselves do not set a good example from within their own organisations, with the 'glass ceiling' continuing to prevent women from making full use of their abilities and reaching senior management positions. Development agencies are wary of releasing figures on the gender makeup of their staff but a background note from the World Bank in 1995 states that in that year, with women comprising 51 per cent of all staff employed, 30 per cent of professional staff, 23 per cent of advanced professional staff, 12 per cent of management and eight per cent of senior management were women (World Bank, 1995b). These figures were the result of a significant effort to promote women within the Bank since 1988, when

> interviews with managers and senior staff revealed 'subconscious but powerful attitudes and actions' that created stereotypes about women's ability to lead, and barriers to recruitment and promotion (World Bank, 1995b, p1).

The image projected to the outside world therefore continues to be one where important decisions, including those relating to development initiatives with women, are made by men. Exhortations to developing countries to improve the representation of women in public life and in the high status professions sounds a little hollow in this context. The same can be said of NGOs, where there is only now emerging a recognition of the need to change internal structures so as to allow for appropriate female role models to emerge which can be presented to beneficiaries as examples of what women can do. It is not easy to talk about gender equity when there are few (or no) women in positions of responsibility within your own organisation.

Conclusion

In conclusion, the development agencies' literature and activities surrounding the promotion of women's education can be summed up as supporting women, firstly as reproducers and only secondly as producers. While agency awareness of gender issues is improving, to date there are very few programmes which promote women as leaders and decision-makers. Donors have been so preoccupied with getting more girls enrolled in school that they have ignored the role that schooling plays in perpetuating traditional attitudes towards male and female roles in society. Given that few efforts have been made to change attitudes in the school and outside, it is not surprising that the task of closing the gender gap in education so as to meet the goal of universal primary education by the year 2000 has proved difficult. Parental perceptions of the limited benefits of educating girls to the same level as boys remain unchanged, and the low profile of women in the labour market merely serves to confirm prevailing attitudes of women's role in society.

And yet education can play a vital role in changing attitudes. An undifferentiated and gender sensitive curriculum which offers a broad range of career opportunities to girls, teaching and learning materials which actively seek to promote an image of girls as good at mathematics and sciences, and teacher education programmes which eliminate conscious and unconscious stereotyping among both male and female teachers are vital in this respect. Much has been done in terms of eliminating gender bias within schooling in some Western nations and the investment is beginning to pay off in terms of numbers of females studying at higher levels in traditional male subject areas and taking a greater share of high status jobs. Donors need to learn lessons from this experience and to fund programmes which seek to influence the socialisation process within schools in developing countries so that they serve ultimately to transform and empower.

Notes

1. The World Bank is of course not a donor or aid agency insofar as it only provides loans not grants. With regard to the poorest countries, these loans are provided by the International Development Association wing of the World Bank on highly preferential terms, with up to 40 years repayment period and very low interest rates. The terms 'aid' and 'donor' are used very loosely here, to include the development banks as well as the aid agencies.

2. *Editors' note*: We are reminded of Oliver Sacks' account of the deaf who were outraged when, in response to their request for practice in job interviews, all the arrangements were made for them. This they said was what they needed to learn how to do just as much as taking part in the interview itself. Anything less was patronising and demeaning (Students at Galludet, reported in 'Seeing Voices').

References

Anand, A. (1993) *The Power to Change: A Report by the Women's Feature Service*. London: Zed.

Acker, S. (1987) Feminist theory and the study of Gender and Education. In *International Review of Education*, XXXIII, 419-435.

Appleton, H. (ed.) (1995) *Do It Herself: Women and Technical Innovation*. London: Intermediate Technology.

Boeh-Ocansey, O. (1995) 'Ghana Country Study' in Leach, F. (ed) *Education and Training for the Informal Sector*, Volume 2: Country Studies. Education Research Serial No. 11, Overseas Development Administration. London.

British Broadcasting Corporation (BBC) (1994) *Breaking Glass*. London: BBC Education.

Buvinic, M. (1986) Projects for Women in the Third World: explaining their misbehaviour. In *World Development*. Vol. 14, No. 5, pp 653-664.

Davies, L. (1992) School Power Cultures under Economic Constraint. In *Educational Review*, Vol. 44, No. 2, pp127-136.

Davison, J. and Kanyuka, M. (1992) Girls' participation in basic education in Southern Malawi. In *Comparative Education review*, Vol. 36, No. 4, pp 446-466.

Deem, R. (ed.) (1980) *Schooling for Women's Work*. London: Routledge.

Duncan, W.A. (1989) *Engendering School Learning: Science, Attitudes and Achievement among Girls and Boys in Botswana*. Institute of International Education, University of Stockholm. Stockholm.

Ellis, P. (1990) *Measures Increasing the Participation of Girls and Women in Technical and Vocational Education and Training: A Caribbean Study*. London: Commonwealth Secretariat.

Goodale, G. (1989) Training for women in the informal sector. In F. Fluitman (ed.) *Training for Work in the Informal Sector*. Geneva: ILO, 47-71.

Gordon, R. (1995) *Causes of Girls' Academic Under-Achievement: the Influence of Teachers' Attitudes and Expectations on the Academic Performance of Secondary School Girls*. Occasional paper No. 8, Human Resources Research Centre, Faculty of Education University of Zimbabwe.

Harding, J. (1992) *Breaking the Barrier: Girls in Science Education*. Paris: IIEP.

ILO (1992) *Increasing Women's Participation in Technical Fields*. Geneva: International Labour Office.

King, E.M. and Hill M.A. (1993) *Women's Education in Developing Countries: Barriers, Benefits and Policies*. Washington DC: World Bank.

Leach, F. (1996) Women in the informal sector: the contribution of education and training. In *Development in Practice*, 6, pp125-136.

Mbilinyi, M. and Mgughuni, P. (eds) (1991) *Education in Tanzania with a Gender Perspective: Summary report*. SIDA (Swedish International Development Authority), Education Division Documents No. 53. Stockholm.

Odaga, A. and Heneveld, W. (1995) *Girls and Schools in Sub-Saharan Africa: From Analysis to Action*. World Bank Technical Paper Number 298. Washington DC: World Bank.

Ouston, J. (ed.) (1993) *Women in Education Management*. Harlow: Longman.

Stromquist, N. (1994) *Gender and Basic Education in International Development Cooperation*. New York: UNICEF.

Rogers, A. (1994) *Women, Literacy, Income Generation*. Reading: Education for Development.

Sacks, O. (1989) *Seeing Voices*: New York. Stoddart.

Tietjen, K. (1991) *Educating Girls: Strategies to Increase Access, Persistence and Achievement.* ABEL Project. Washington DC: USAID.

UNESCO (1996) *Education for All: Achieving the Goal.* Mid-Decade Meeting of the International Consultative Forum on Education for All 16-19 June, Amman, Jordan.

United Nations (1995) *The World's Women: Trends and Statistics.* New York: United Nations.

WCEFA (1990) *World Conference on Education for All: Meeting Basic Learning Needs* 5-9 March 1990, Jomtien, Thailand. Final Report. New York: Inter-agency Commission, WCEFA.

World Bank (1991) *Vocational and Technical Education and Training: A World Bank Policy Paper.* Washington DC: World Bank.

World Bank (1995a) *Priorities and Strategies for Education: A World Bank Review.* Washington DC: World Bank.

World Bank (1995b) Background note: The World Bank Reviews its Commitment to 'Excellence Through Equality'. *Women in the World Bank* Washington DC: World Bank.

Chapter 5

Non-formal primary education: a gender-based programme

Zeeshan H. Rahman

Bangladesh in South Asia covers an area of 147,570 square kilometres and is populated by about 120 million people. Of this vast population only 35.3 per cent are literate.

The Bangladesh Rural Advancement Committee, now known as BRAC, began in 1972 as a small committee to carry out emergency activities in Sylhet immediately after the devastating war of liberation. Houses were rebuilt with BRAC bamboo poles and livelihoods were restored with BRAC fishing boats and nets. At that time it was intended that the Committee should last no longer than the return of the refugees to their homes. However it was soon clear that rural needs went far beyond simple relief and reconstruction. Poverty, disease, ignorance and exploitation were endemic throughout the countryside. Touched by that first experience in Sylhet, few of those early BRAC workers ever returned to their jobs in the private sector and government offices. Eventually BRAC emerged as a 'rehabilitation committee', then 'rural advancement committee', and finally just BRAC, transforming itself into the biggest non-governmental organisation in the world. In Bangladesh BRAC has become synonymous with efficiency, effectiveness and all the best meanings that can be attached to the word 'development'. BRAC's programmes now are largely dedicated to improving conditions for disadvantaged women.

Eighty per cent of Bangladesh's female population live in the rural areas, so no real development can take place if women are not involved. Until women are educated, any attempt to improve their economic conditions and establish their social and political rights will be of no use. This is because socio-cultural realities have to be taken into account. In traditional rural society in Bangladesh, girl children are always discriminated against qualitatively as well as materially. Girls are not encouraged to express their own needs and opinions and to make demands is a sign of bad upbringing. For daughters, the ultimate purpose of education is marriage and the successful discharge of the roles of daughter-in-law, wife and mother. For sons it means developing the ability to earn a living, marry and produce children and to become respectable members of society. Women receive a poorer education than men; they have little access to and security of land tenure and very limited opportunity to obtain conventional agricultural credit. Integrating women in all development efforts is one of the most difficult tasks in such a culture, where girls are often kept inside the house, with no chance to work outside. They may be married at the age of 13 or even younger. Denied basic rights to literacy and numeracy they are then virtually imprisoned for the rest of their lives.

This is a major problem in Bangladesh: inappropriate and inadequate local schools for girls with parents reluctant to send girls far from their homes for schooling. As a result girls are likely either never to enrol in school, or to drop out of education.

BRAC currently (1997) runs three programmes: Rural Development Programme; Health and Population Division; and Non-Formal Primary Education (NFPE). In this chapter I shall only briefly describe the first two programmes before developing a more detailed discussion of Non-Formal Primary Education and how it has raised issues which demonstrate the extent to which gender awareness must permeate the whole organisation if it is to meet its aims of educating girls and women to basic levels of literacy.

The Rural Development Programme gives credit to the members of Village Organisations, mainly (90 per cent) women, for projects like poultry farming, fisheries, irrigation, sericulture, rural enterprise projects, social forestry and vegetable and maize cultivation. Free training is also given in these areas. A legal education programme, the Human Rights and Legal Education Programme, was started in 1986, based on the assumption that legal awareness would help members of village organisations protect themselves against illegal, unfair or discriminatory practices. In 1997 there were 1.8 million members in almost 54,000 village organisations participating in the Rural Development Programme, 90 per cent of them women involved in poultry projects. Collectively they had saved over one million Taka, which is about 30 million US dollars. In 1996 they borrowed over five million Taka (128 million US dollars) for productive enterprises, repaying virtually all of it on time.

The main objectives of BRAC's Health and Population Division are to improve the fitness and nutritional status of women and children through health initiatives, and by developing and strengthening the capacity of communities to sustain these initiatives. An estimated 12 million women and children are covered by BRAC's Health and Population Programmes.

Non-Formal Primary Education Programme

In response to the needs of the rural poor, especially girls, BRAC pioneered a Non-Formal Primary Education Programme in 1985, to complement formal schooling. Instituted in response to a mother in a Functional Literacy Class who asked staff whether her children would have to wait until they were 18 to join the school, the programme started with 22 experimental schools. Today, BRAC runs 34,400 schools, catering for more than a million students. The students at BRAC schools are the children of the poor and landless. They are the 'unreachable' who have been denied education because of gender or poverty. At least 70 per cent of the children enrolled in schools are girls. BRAC has always emphasised the creation of an environment which would gradually lead to equal education opportunities for both boys and girls. Almost all teachers on the programme are female, as parents prefer this for their daughters. This helps to retain more girls in school. It also helps women teachers make social changes in their own right. They report being easily recognised in their community and having people talk to them eagerly and with respect. Moreover, earning an income of their own is empowering and gives independence.

The schools

BRAC currently operates two different school models. In 1985, the Non-Formal Primary Education model was started as a three year programme for children between the ages of 8 and 10. In 1988 Basic Education for Older Children through *Kishor Kishori* Schools began. These schools enabled students aged 11-14 or slightly older to attend school. Schooling also lasts for three years, but progress through the curriculum is accelerated so that students can cover the equivalent of five academic years' worth of material.

There is a Scholarship Programme for students with the potential for successful completion of mid-level (Standard 8). Those gaining the award should be female, but exceptions may be made should a boy hold a record of outstanding class performance, and come from a background which meets the economic criteria for selection, i.e. one of very limited means.

The curriculum

There has recently been a change in the Non-Formal Primary Education curriculum. Gender is a major focus, especially in the new Social Studies curriculum which aims to highlight certain social dimensions to male and female behaviour in order to help young children, both girls and boys, develop wider perspectives than older generations. In Year I gender is considered in the context of the family. The message put forward is that when the brother helps his sister with household chores, it frees time for the girl to attend school. In Year II students discuss the concept of paid and unpaid labour in order to help them understand that work done by the women in the family is often not acknowledged or is taken for granted as it is unpaid. Gender in Year III deals with profiles of great women. Illustrations have also been carefully chosen to provide gender-sensitised contexts free from conventional stereotyping. For instance a father washing his daughter's hands before eating or a girl going to the market would be quite unusual in real life in Bangladesh, but these scenarios are included.

Language and mathematics books are also using more female characters in stories and illustrations. *Meena* was developed as a project for the Decade of the Girl Child in South Asia. An animated film series and story books highlighting Meena's exploits have been developed by UNICEF to inspire girls, their families and communities across all sectors of South Asian society. The Social Studies curriculum has also carefully considered the use of *Meena* in the topics covered.

Schools for ex-garment workers

BRAC is collaborating with UNICEF, the International Labour Organisation (ILO) and the Bangladesh Garment Manufacturers and Exporters Association to provide schooling for ex-garment workers, under the age of 14. 2,200 child labourers are studying in these schools. These students receive a payment of Taka 300 as a scholarship.

Libraries, Reading Circles and Literacy Centres

In order to maintain interest in reading and access to books, libraries have been established for graduates from BRAC schools. These are specifically targeted at young women, many of whom marry after their three years basic education, and who, without opportunity, lose the skills and interest they acquired at school. Libraries also serve as meeting places and training centres; in 1994 some new activities were introduced such as training in vegetable and home gardening, in poultry farming and in tailoring. They are also successful in attracting young women to meet and socialise informally. To facilitate a reading environment in the rural areas, BRAC has also opened village libraries. Each library is equipped with about a thousand books, newspapers and journals. The numbers of women using these libraries is steadily increasing.

Reading circles were developed in 1995 as a strategy to support reading in areas where there were no BRAC schools to support a library, or where there were not enough members to warrant a full library. As a result, small reading or study groups with a minimum of five members in each group were formed with a contact person chosen from the group. There are now 1,165 such study groups in existence with 7,573 girls as members. The participants are mostly those continuing their education in formal schools with girls and women who are not studying in school any longer, but still wish to go on with their reading.

The Non-Formal Primary Education programme also includes illiterate adults in its ambit, through literacy centres. Each centre aims to place 25 learners with a single teacher. These centres have a rapidly growing membership, which increased fourfold in the three months up to the end of March 1996. They are now up to capacity in terms of teacher-student ratio, and without an increase in the number of centres and teachers, there is a danger that the demand for places will outstrip the available facilities.

Gender initiatives in BRAC

In the early years the number of women staff working for BRAC was negligible. Gender issues seemed less important than emergency practical relief. Since the mid 1980s, BRAC has undergone a tremendous expansion in area coverage and staff strength. Many women were recruited in 1990, but it was one thing to recruit women and quite another to retain them. Many left because of dissatisfaction with the organisation, their place in it and the difficulties they were experiencing as women employees. The organisation at the time had no means of listening to the issues, questions and complaints being voiced by these women in private, and many vacated posts were filled by men who were not used to dealing with women staff, thus compounding the problem.

A Women's Advisory Committee was created in 1991 to begin the process of dialogue between women and men staff and to help BRAC management understand gender issues. The Women's Committee has conducted a number of workshops with a sample of female staff around the country. The Committee also periodically interviews staff on gender-related concerns for its internal publications and programming work. It was thus possible to identify specific concerns facing women in the organisation. Today the organisation has around 18,000 staff and more than 33,000 part-time teachers in villages throughout Bangladesh. Since 1990 BRAC's commitment to gender equity is demonstrated in the increase in numbers of women staff, currently 23 per cent of the total workforce, and rising. Women's views and opinions regarding their professional development are now given priority. There is strong executive support for the recruitment and promotion of women. For example, it was decided by the top executives that if at all possible, only women will be recruited from the year 1995, and among the three core programmes two are headed by women.

General problems faced by the female field staff

Women employees of BRAC have had to deal with a range of problems which their male colleagues have not had to face. In many of these cases, BRAC has been able to propose and generally to implement workable solutions.

Lack of a professional background has meant for some BRAC workers that such activities as writing reports and presenting papers in seminars and conferences can be really daunting. Male staff seem to be able to use unofficial networks to learn from colleagues. Women in equal need of such support are more likely to miss out on information sharing and informal mutual help from within the organisation, as they are in the minority in most departments. Recognition by BRAC of this state of affairs has led to women employees being specifically encouraged to attend national and international courses for their professional development.

The location of work postings also poses particular problems for some women. Some find themselves allocated to areas remote from home, and as women are still expected to take a significant lead in domestic management and labour, whether or not they work outside the home, distant postings make their dual role untenable. Such problems can undoubtedly be exacerbated even further, if married couples working in BRAC are transferred to different places for work. Simple attention to recruitment procedures and a degree of sensitivity has helped to deal with both of these problems: these days, women are recruited locally and asked if they want to be stationed near to their home; a management ruling is now in place throughout BRAC recognising that married employees must be posted to the same or nearby offices. It is made clear that BRAC's women employees' assumed domestic skills are not to be exploited at work. Women and men are now prohibited from having any involvement in preparing meals, under a code of conduct requiring each BRAC office to have a cook in the kitchen. Thus, women employees should no longer be expected to cook for visitors.

Moreover, BRAC has made it clear that women employees have just as much right as their male colleagues to move around freely and independently outside the confines of the camp office during the weekly holidays as well as throughout the working day. It is now a requirement that constraints such as curfews and camp rules are not to be applied to women working for BRAC.

Problems experienced by women workers specifically linked to issues of reproductive health and welfare have also been tackled with more or less success by BRAC as an important management issue.

Separate bathroom facilities have been provided for female staff in all field offices, and women who wish to do so are allowed to stop travelling by bicycle in the course of their work for three days during menstruation. However, this situation has not been resolved satisfactorily in that it still gives rise to embarrassment for some women because they have to approach male supervisors for the necessary permission. Some readers might well feel outraged that women should be put in such a humiliating position dressed up as an emancipated concession to women at work.

Maternity leave has been extended so that in addition to three months paid leave of absence for new mothers, six months unpaid leave is also granted following the birth, with a further three months unremunerated entitlement available to be taken at any time during pregnancy. Moreover, staff at the Gender Research Centre (GRC) are able to make use of a crèche recently set up at the head office; it is hoped that this will make it less likely that women staff will have to leave their jobs if there is no one at home to take care of the child.

These examples show how, when specific issues are identified, action can be taken to bring about change. However, far from solving every problem, the Women's Advisory Committee also found that behavioural changes were needed among the staff. As a result the Training Division incorporated gender-sensitisation awareness into the staff training course. A session was included in the training course, under the title *Men's and Women's Relationships in Development Work*. It rapidly became clear that the two-hour session could not possibly address all training needs. As a result a separate Gender Awareness and Analysis course was introduced in 1994. Unfortunately the course did not have any means of following up issues, once workers were away in the field, so external consultants were brought in to assess gender needs. Four senior trainers worked alongside the consultants for a year and as a result a gender team was formed in the organisation in 1994. The team initiated a Gender Quality Action Learning Programme which aims to:

* improve the quality of programme with village women

* improve gender relations within BRAC

* provide valid data for gender-related strategic planning by the managers

* provide an orientation on gender issues to a cross-section of staff.

The key initial intervention in the process is provided through Gender Quality Seminars which give BRAC staff the knowledge and skills to take action for gender improvements. This learning programme has been specially tailored to meet the needs of BRAC. The team conducted a series of workshops in 1994 with over 400 BRAC staff from various divisions and levels. It also surveyed staff to ascertain different perspectives on gender issues. As a consequence, to support this programme a Gender Resource Centre was also set up, the main objective being to provide information and a place for women staff to come together and talk about their concerns.

Management staff also need to be gender aware so all team leaders and senior programme organisers attend a six day Gender Awareness and Analysis Course which addresses a wide range of gender-related issues essential to the programme.

The programme has changed its recruitment policy to encourage women to apply for different posts. Vacancies are now advertised in local newspapers as well as nationally. Affirmative action policy in place since 1995 ensures that only if a post cannot be filled by a woman will a man be offered it. Since 1995 about 270 women have been recruited as staff into NFPE; at present 15.4 per cent staff are women. Some women have also been promoted rapidly in order to narrow the gap between the numbers of male and female staff at management level.

As much of BRAC activity is carried out in rural areas by field workers, it is important that policy is understood and implemented in the field. The surveys have been illuminating in revealing the thinking of field staff.

Voices of the field staff

Understanding of empowerment issues is still rudimentary at field level. Field staff recognise standard gender differences such as women's lack of education and power; they do not probe causal factors and often make statements suggesting that differences are intrinsic to women and men, or that women are responsible for their situation – e.g. 'women are weaker than men' and 'women are less risk-taking.' The perceptions of some health workers, acknowledging for instance that 'even though women contribute to household income, men own the assets purchased', or 'though men and women both work, men think they work harder', are rare. Women area managers tend to be more analytical: they may say that 'society perceives women primarily as child-bearers and rearers who should stay behind boundary walls and who are meant to serve as objects of male enjoyment.' In contrast, comparable male managers comment that 'women's movements are restricted', or 'women are physically weak so they cannot perform all jobs'. Women noted that 'men think women work less and therefore devalue their work', and that 'men think they are superior.'

Conclusion

Inevitably BRAC is struggling to cross barriers constructed as a result of cultural, religious and social norms, which take a long time to change, especially in a society which is strongly patriarchal, and where women do not have a public voice in the affairs of the community. Within this society BRAC has successfully worked as a bridge for the girls to continue their studies and join government schools. This progress has been made because of the success of the students on the NFPE programme. Changed perceptions give the strength to make decisions on their own. Not only students but also parents acquire a broader outlook towards their own daughters. Seeing their daughters gain from education has also helped them see their daughters in a different light. Though many still want them married as soon as possible, it is also becoming a possibility for girls to continue their studies. Large numbers of female teachers also feel that they are respected by the community and can contribute to their family's income.

BRAC is a large wide-ranging organisation and so encompasses widely different practices. To the outside world, the organisation is radical. At the policy level, direct strategies are implemented to increase the number of women workers at all levels within the organisation, and support is provided in order to retain them. In its day-to day practice BRAC often appears to operate counter-culturally, requiring women workers to do unconventional activities, for instance riding bicycles and motorcycles. This is rather unusual in a society where women are supposed to stay at home and do housework. Women staff generally feel strong enough to deal with criticism from villagers about such practices and profess themselves unconcerned by it. Moreover these women have managed to break the norms of behaviour and by doing so help to create a level of acceptance of their new activities in the communities. However conditions within BRAC are different. The women field staff believe that senior BRAC male staff undermine women and that women's capabilities are not recognised. They also think that women are weaker in management, less capable of arguing logically and cannot work as hard as men.

BRAC as an organisation serves as a good example of how gendered behaviour at work is socially and culturally constructed. The aim of educating girls and women translated into practice is seen to have direct impact on the conditions of the individuals bringing about that change, through a redefinition of working practices. The women workers are essential for the bringing about of change, because of the nature of the cultural shifts which are desired, yet are themselves subject to cultural forces within the society. The organisation is also recognising that gender awareness is a necessary part of its own internal framework.

References

Bangladesh Rural Advancement Committee (1996) *NFPE Phase One Report*, January 1993 to March 1996. BRAC Dhaka.

Bangladesh Rural Advancement Committee (1994) *Non-Formal Primary Education Annual Report 1994*. BRAC Dhaka.

UNICEF *Meena* animated film series, produced in collaboration with Hanna-Barbera Productions and Ram Mohan Studios. Dhaka.

Section Three
Women as Managers

Women do make it into management, in education as in other areas of work, and we tend to believe this to be more so in education than most other professions. Of course these successes should be celebrated and emulated, but they also need to be scrutinised.

The final three chapters of this collection present viewpoints from women who have 'made it' into management; who are now on the inside looking out and perhaps upwards, to follow men to the higher reaches of power and influence. Each outlines one social, cultural and political backdrop against which women managers operate. Indonesia, the West Indies and South Africa seem to share some affinities, as the experiences of these women suggest.

There are three main themes. Firstly, professions are compared, to explore an apparently world-wide assumption that education is 'women-friendly'. Second, the nature of the lives of working women at managerial levels is examined in relation to domestic responsibility. The third theme is a consequence of the previous two. The authors present their observations, research and personal stories to help us to understand how they have achieved their success.

Chrysanti Hasibuan-Sedyono reveals a picture by no means unique to Indonesia, of a growing number of women arriving in the workforce, but clustered around the lowest income levels and with poor prospects, conditions and status. Those who do achieve high positions are shown to be under continual threat: of no further promotion; of losing respect because of insufficient attention to their families. She compares education and banking as the domains of women managers and reviews the legislation.

Legislation purporting to support women in the Indonesian labour force is considered, showing how legislation and employment practices discriminate both directly and indirectly against women workers.

Tensions for women in Indonesia between domestic and employment roles, and issues surrounding the sexual division of labour are also made explicit. These are seen however, as the personal and private concerns of individuals. Middle class women are helped by the availability of cheap domestic labour and support from the extended family but prevailing orthodoxies in Indonesian society as to the behaviour and roles appropriate to women, particularly married women, constrain the activities of the relatively few such 'career women'. Unremitting prejudice is evident at all levels, from the executive boardroom to the family home. What Chrysanti Hasibuan-Sedyono terms 'tradeoffs' seem inevitable for career women who want to 'have it all'.

Jeanette Morris tackles similar issues through her study of school principals in the West Indies. Observing that women principals tend to be in single-sex academic girls' schools, and in the context of schools in the West Indies being re-organised into mixed-sex comprehensives, she wonders whether women will be less likely to become principals in the future. She investigates the career trajectories of successful women, looking at what motivated them to try for senior posts, and whether they brought with them particular management concepts or strategies.

Characteristics and personal histories of successful women managers are cited, and between them, Chrysanti Hasibuan-Sedyono and Jeanette Morris offer us almost a list of the attributes and the social situations of successful women in education. But they diverge on the question of ability. Naively, perhaps even touchingly, in the light of the data presented by Chrysanti Hasibuan-Sedyono, Indonesian women appear to believe that ability, rather than gender or anything else, is the determinant of success. Jeanette Morris, on the other hand, offers accounts where the women themselves did not consider themselves able or well-placed to strive for promotion.

A couple of the Caribbean women claim to have sought promotion to escape the stresses and strains of classroom teaching. Senior administrative posts were seen to be 'easier' by these teachers but we do not know whether it implies less work, or more stimulating work, or whether it aligns with these particular women's view of themselves. This would provide an interesting starting point for further study, and is of particular interest in the light of work by Kathleen Casey reported in Goodson (1992) on activist, radical women teachers who leave teaching altogether because of their dislike of the classroom and of the demands of educational administrators.

It is in the West Indian context too that we observe the problems some male teachers have in dealing with women as authority figures. Nonetheless, Jeanette Morris's study indicates successful women in education having happy and supportive families, and work colleagues who trust and encourage them. These women are experienced and academically well-qualified. They reject the idea that 'toughness', meaning insensitivity, is essential to good management, and operate a philosophy of negotiation and participative approaches.

Devarakshanam Betty Govinden views the situation that seems to prevail in all the workplaces discussed in this book, i.e. under-representation at senior levels, from a personal and feminist perspective. She creates a discourse which integrates the personal and professional in the heightened political context of South Africa. Through her account of her time as Dean in the Faculty of Education at the historically black University of Durban-Westville we learn how one successful woman succeeded in integrating her working practices together with herself. Statistics she presents about the uneven gender-composition of senior management at the university affirm the evidence from Indonesia, so much so that when she was invited to become Dean she felt that she had no choice but to 'put her money where her mouth was' and accept. Her account lucidly traces her transition from critic of the system to key player in its management at a crucial point in history.

References
Casey, K. (1992) 'Why do Progressive Women Activists leave Teaching? Theory, Methodology and Politics in Life History Research.' in Goodson, I.F. (ed) (1992) *Studying Teachers' Lives*. New York. Teachers College Press.

Chapter 6

She who manages: the Indonesian woman in management

Chrysanti Hasibuan-Sedyono

Introduction

Women managers are making their mark on Indonesia's male dominated management scene. They can be found in a wide variety of organisations, from multinationals to small-sized businesses; from large Government agencies to tiny voluntary organisations. The trend, which spans sectors and fields traditionally identified as male domains, is irreversible.

Indeed the sounds of the shattering glass ceiling have been heard in many organisations as the 40 per cent of Indonesian women who are in the work force have slowly and gradually gained management positions.

The road to managerial success in Indonesia is nonetheless fraught with difficulties imposed by traditional cultural values. The average Indonesian woman manager still has to cope with conflicting demands which arise from her activities as an executive, and as a wife and mother. This chapter features the Indonesian woman manager's profile, experiences and managerial practices. I have used various sources as references:

* statistics gathered from Indonesian Central Bureau of Statistics reports[1] and the International Labour Organisation (ILO)

* Asian Institute of Management (AIM) surveys[2] from 1987-1989 recorded data which helped to construct profiles and experiences of

women managers in three settings across five countries, corporations; Government, and non-profit organisations in Philippines, Thailand, Malaysia, Singapore and Indonesia.

- a survey of women managers conducted in 1996 in preparation for writing this chapter[3]

Indonesian women in the work force

Since 1945 various initiatives have led to improvements in women's role in society. There is now a Minister of State whose business it is to encourage gender equality. Women's participation in the work force has increased from 12.5 million in 1971 to 38.4 million in 1995.

The agricultural sector continues to absorb large numbers of female workers. Men seem to be moving from agriculture to other opportunities but women have also made inroads into trade, as this does not demand specialised qualifications or capital to get started.

Spectacular employment growth has occurred in the manufacturing sector (73 per cent increase between 1980 and 1990). New job opportunities have been created primarily for younger women in the urban areas, mainly in female labour-intensive industries such as textiles, electronics, food and cigarettes.

Statistics for the service sector show that this may be an even more significant route for increasing women's earnings and economic status. In the 'Restaurants and Hotels' sub-sector the number of females per hundred males increased from 79 to 97; in banking and finance from 21 to 34; and in government service, communications and personal services from 38 to 61: all in the decade 1980 to 1990.[4]

While economic factors are significant, there have also been regional differences in female labour participation in Indonesia. The country's various ethnic groups traditionally impose differing degrees of constraint upon women working outside the home. Bali has the highest level of female workforce participation (64.5 per cent), since Balinese women have traditionally contributed to the family's economy through productive work within and outside the household. Women in Sulawesi and the Sudanese women of West Java, in contrast to their Javanese counterparts from East Java, are not traditionally encouraged to take paid employment outside the home.

The women consistently earn less than men. Central Bureau of Statistics figures relating to 3,296 establishments across Indonesia show that on average the daily wages of unskilled women workers in 1990 were less than two-thirds those of men of similar skill (CBS 1991-5). The World Bank Survey of March 1991 also confirmed that women are paid far less than men in the same age group and educational category, and among administrative, non-production workers, males earn about a quarter more than females.

Discrimination

Legally there are no constraints on women's employment in Indonesia. Indeed on paper Indonesian Labour Laws are among the most advanced in the world in supporting women's struggle for equal rights and opportunities. In reality, several instances of discriminatory practice can be reported.

Working women have maternity leave of six weeks before and six weeks after giving birth, as well as a so-called menstruation leave of 3 days in a month. This is sometimes interpreted as an extra gift of 17 weeks plus 3 days in a year[5] to working women! (Susanto, 1988) and is often used as an excuse for not assigning an important post to a woman because of concern for lower productivity.

Physical constraints affecting, for example, women's ability to work on construction projects are using as another excuse for not employing men and women equally[6]. A regulation prohibiting women workers from working night shift has induced certain companies to hire fewer women. One extraordinary case in 1988 occurred at a textile factory which employed men until they reached the age of 55 but made the women workers retire at 40. This discrimination led the National Board of the Indonesian Women's Congress (a federation of women's organisations) to question this practice with the Minister of Manpower. Eventually the Labour Union officers (who were all male) replied that the legislation was designed to *protect* the women workers who had to stand continuously while working and were only allowed to rest for half an hour a day (Suara Karya, 1988).

Another obvious discrimination is that married women in Indonesia are generally regarded as single in their work place. This means they do not get any family allowances. These go to the men, the rationale being that men are the main wage-earners, so the income which women earn is just supplementary. Worse still, there are cases where women have to sign contracts which contain a clause to the effect that their employment will be terminated in case of marriage or pregnancy.

More women work in lower positions than men as factory workers or secretaries. This makes them vulnerable to sexual harassment by superiors. Women in higher positions tend to be older and their age and superior status offer some protection from such sexual aggression.

So the gap between *de jure* and *de facto* discrimination against women in Indonesia is still quite wide, due mainly to the influence of traditional social attitudes and customs.

Indonesian women are active in almost all sectors of employment. However, traditionally the woman is still expected to be wife and mother, to keep house and bring up the children.

Women's maternal and domestic roles and responsibilities are officially recognised in Indonesia. This is commendable but over-emphasis on this can do much harm if women's activities are deemed insignificant, and their earnings seen as secondary sources of family income. Men are still considered the primary breadwinners in Indonesia. It is likely that working women are also mothers. This raises troubling socio-cultural questions, not only in Indonesia but also in other Southeast Asian countries. Shouldn't women be at home taking care of the children? Indeed, should women have careers at all? Does it push men out of their traditional place? Southeast Asian men and women are still considering the implications of these issues in the privacy of their homes and in the secrecy of their own minds.

Indonesian women at work
In education, which in keeping with other countries is regarded as women-friendly, there were in 1990 28,538 female lecturers or 20.2 per cent out of a total of 141,094 in higher education institutions. Among these were 44 female Presidents out of 780 (5.6 per cent) altogether and

73 female Deans out of 1038 (7 per cent) altogether. In 1970 and 1980 the comparative figures for women were negligible. In Indonesia about 80 per cent of those possessing a doctoral degree were surveyed in 1995 by the Ministry of Education. Among these 2956 PhD.s, only one in ten women was a university professor, despite women constituting a quarter of the sample[7] So the friendliness of education towards women becomes distinctly cool as women actually gain the qualifications to take up senior positions.

The picture in another women-friendly sector, the banking industry, has shown an interesting shift. In 1983, out of a total of 200 directors of private banks, only five were women (2.5 per cent), but of 475 directors in 1992 there were 40 women (8 per cent). Even more striking is the number of women branch managers: there were only 1.5 per cent (three persons) in 1983 but by 1992 this had jumped to a figure of 17 per cent or 198 persons (Infobank, 1993).

The phenomenon of women working outside their homes is still new in Indonesia, so society follows the movements of career women with considerable interest, one might say with a magnifying glass, quick to judge whether the ways women conduct their working lives are appropriate within existing norms, and whether they properly maintain their position as caring and nurturing wives and mothers. The stereotype of a woman in Indonesia is a creature who is emotional, passive, weak, dependent, decorative, obedient, unassertive and incompetent except for household tasks. Husbands should be the wage earners, responsible for the family and hence have higher status and be in control.

This viewpoint is especially prevalent in Javanese society, Javanese people being the biggest distinctive ethnic group in Indonesia. Women are called 'konco wingking' (a companion who walks behind someone) and there is even a saying 'swargo nunut neroko katut' (going to heaven or hell, a woman will merely go along with her husband). A Javanese woman is supposed to remember that cooking, being well-groomed and giving birth to children are her main tasks, and she should think very carefully before deciding to pursue a career.

If a woman does work outside her home, very often she has to listen to her husband's or parents' views about what is appropriate. An article

(*Asian Business*, 1993) about working women in a number of Asian countries described how the Director for Credit and Marketing of a big company in Indonesia intended to send one of her woman subordinates to a training programme in Singapore but could not get the approval of her husband. Likewise, a Public Relations manager of a large international hotel was not allowed by her parents to undertake business trips to other Asian countries. A high-ranking (male) official of a national committee[8] stated that Indonesian women government officials who are single are usually energetic, productive and enjoy challenging jobs, but once they are married those positive traits tend to deteriorate (*Warta Ekonomi*, 1993).

Indonesian society still closely relates family welfare with the mother. Faced with a highly successful career woman, people will ask: 'How is her family doing?' whereas men never have to face this kind of question. And if by any chance the family of the said successful career woman is in a less than ideal situation, she will be ruthlessly condemned as a failure.

Indonesian society still insists that women have not completed their mission in life until they have married and have brought up children. Problems for women result from trying to deal with role conflicts or social pressures resulting from simply having too much to do. However, the availability of household help and baby-sitters at relatively low salaries makes it easier for women executives to pursue their careers, as does the extended family system. This benefit to a few high status women is at the expense of the many others supporting them from poorly paid positions that offer little hope of career advancement.

One successful women manager confessed to me that when her children were very young she used to wake up at five o 'clock in the morning so that she could prepare the food her husband and her children liked. She said that this helped substantially to reduce the guilt she felt about working long hours outside the home.

An article in '*Eksekutif*' magazine described how a high-ranking official of a state-owned company opined that a woman playing multiple roles is of 'higher value' as a woman, because she is contributing to the family as well as to the economy of the nation (Darsa and

Rizal, 1990). Is this is a minority view? According to Professor Ihromi from the Centre of Women's Studies, University of Indonesia, most of the 95 middle class men in Jakarta questioned in a study, reacted positively towards the statement 'a married woman may work outside home'. However, only 40 per cent of them had working wives (Ihromi, 1990). One interpretation of this might be that the majority of husbands in Indonesia believe: 'It is all right for a women to work outside the home, as long as she is not my wife!'

In Indonesia, women executives still experience obstacles in their environment, such as old-fashioned prejudices like the 'lady supervisor means trouble', or myths and stereotyping about gender roles which typecast women into nurturing, supporting types of jobs. It often happens that management systems, deliberately or not, assume that women are too emotional, not tough enough, can't make decisions, are not aggressive enough, less committed to their careers and so on, and discriminate accordingly. Women have to work much harder than men because they have to start at a negative point. A respondent in one of the AIM studies clearly described the situation:

> For men, starting at 'zero', and getting to a 'plus' is easier. For women, starting from 'negative point', they have to erase the 'negative' first before they can even get to 'zero'! In this sense, a woman has to prove herself first. She has to work harder to be accepted at the same level as men! (AIM, 1987-89)

And a famous ex-President Director of a leading private Bank in Jakarta declared in an interview:

> ...if I have to choose between two applicants for a job, a man and a woman who have the same capabilities, I will choose the man. A man has an edge, because he is rational. The leaders in this world are mostly men, right? In women emotional feeling will always be there, whereas in our jobs we need to make decisions based on rational thinking, not merely feeling... (Soekarsono, 1994)

It might be an interesting coincidence that not too long after this interview was given, a single woman was selected by the said Bank Board of Directors to replace the speaker as the Bank's President Director!

Women managers cannot avoid being judged as women. They are often measured by two yardsticks: how as women they carry out the management role; and how as managers they live up to images of womanhood. Women who attempt to fit themselves into a managerial role by acting like men risk being condemned as 'too aggressive', or worse, just plain 'bitchy'. Yet those who act like 'ladies' risk being seen as ineffective or simply incapable. For example, the first woman Dean at a Higher Education Institution as well as being appropriately highly qualified and motivated, was also very 'feminine'. She was not criticised for her credentials, but she was accused (by some) of being 'too feminine', and 'too much of a woman'.

Factors behind success

The twenty successful women managers, half of them in education, whom I interviewed recently, mostly attributed their success to hard work, perseverance, determination and competence. The external factors they mentioned most frequently were educational background, support from boss or mentor (those in education sectors also mentioned peers) and contacts made through work. The in-depth interviews revealed that these women managers already showed early signs of leadership, enjoyed challenges and took pride from a job well done. They were personable and good at developing relationships with people; again these traits were shown even when they were at school. They also demonstrated a strong drive to improve themselves.

Although less true of those in education, most of the women managers, particularly the corporate managers, realised they had a high price to pay for their success. They felt their family relationships were at risk. Some felt compelled to give up or postpone starting a family. Social activities were cut down to a minimum, extra time devoted to work.

Some women do not question the importance of family and the primary responsibilities of women to be homemakers: they take the unambiguous view that family responsibilities come first. There is then a genuine acceptance of the need for a trade-off between career and family in which 'family' always prevails. So they are less torn than the others over making a choice between career and family and they do not appear to manifest frustration, unlike their counterparts who resent that they cannot 'have it all'.

Profile of the successful Indonesian women manager

My mother has always wanted to go to school, but her parents saw women's prime role as wife and mother, and prepared her for marriage instead. Therefore she encouraged all her children to get the highest education possible. My father also believed in the highest formal education not only for his sons but also his daughters, though he also insists on us girls learning the domestic chores. (Female Dean of a college)

The AIM surveys revealed that about 80 per cent of the total respondents were university graduates, and all had some form of higher education. Moreover, many had also achieved outstanding results.

Virtually all the women surveyed attributed their educational attainment to parental influence. Even if most of their fathers and mothers had not gone to university they valued education and encouraged their children to pursue academic excellence.

Typically the women in the studies originated from the middle or upper class, and were raised in medium-sized towns or big cities. Their families believed strongly in social values like serving other people and involvement in the community at large. As a respondent who used to be the first woman Rector of a state higher education institution described:

I remember my mother unceasingly telling us that since God blesses us abundantly, we must share it with those who have less. And she regularly distributed cooked meals every Friday to probably all the beggars in town who gathered in our big house-yard!

The hard-working parents of these successful women also stressed discipline and diligence, yet the fathers' and mothers' affection was never in doubt. Since their earliest years, the women surveyed learnt from the family environment a number of things which later proved to be very useful in their careers. Indirectly, the various responsibilities given to them trained or prepared them in planning, budgeting and supervising household tasks, thus enabling them to develop their skills from very early on. Also, even as children, they were given freedom to make certain decisions. They were exposed to interesting people, and they had already dreamed of becoming 'someone important' someday. At 18, the majority thought they knew what they wanted out of life, and many had the type of career or profession pinned down in their mind.

Even those who did not at least knew that they wanted to be something beyond being a good wife and mother.

The women grew up with close family ties. Most spoke about their parents with affection and admiration, expressing gratitude and acknowledgment for their roles in influencing them, for their parents' expectation and encouragement, being role models and for their provision of both emotional and physical support. Their upbringing had inculcated them with a sense of duty to family.

Partners

Eventually, most of the women married and raised children. Their husbands are usually equally highly educated, typically have high positions as managers or professionals, and are the main breadwinners. Their family size is most likely small, with only two or three children; a stark contrast with the big families from which most of the women managers came.

With very few exceptions, the women managers said their husbands were supportive or very supportive of their career. They were virtually unanimous in attributing a major part of their success to this support and encouragement.

Importantly, most of the Indonesian women managers I spoke to showed sensitivity to their husbands' pride and made a point of acknowledging the traditional role of the husband as head of the family and primary wage-earner.[9] Despite their own success they advocated the traditional roles for husbands. The following quote is typical:

> My husband wants to be respected as the eminent person to earn the living. He always says to me that I may have work and activities outside the house as long as I like it, 'but give me the pride to be the breadwinner.' And I absolutely believe he deserves it.

Being dependent on the husband for the family's economic well-being was not considered to imply inequality, but merely an acceptance of tradition. What's more, the women managers often considered it an advantage because it allowed them the luxury of being able to work in areas which gave them personal satisfaction instead of being driven by financial reward[10].

Management styles

The Indonesian women managers interviewed generally found the culture in their working environment to be in line with their personal values. They claimed to practise 'transformational leadership' and were likely to try to use charisma, interpersonal skills and personal contacts to establish team spirit and unleash the creativity, resourcefulness, talent and energy of their employees. They generally claim that their management style is not autocratic, preferring to operate successfully by exerting beneficial influence on those they manage rather than by imposing direct orders[11].

Typically, an Indonesian woman manager would describe her business as a family and see her business relationship as a network. She would take the time to understand other people's behaviour, get to know them, figure out what works for each person, and from there derive the approach to be used. She would share information; working to enhance her subordinates' self-worth and to energise them to feel good about themselves and their work. In other words, she would try to create commitment by empowering employees. However, while demonstrating all of these characteristics, she would also make tough calls whenever necessary to get an important job done and would not be afraid to incur displeasure as long as she believed herself to be right, or when an urgent task had to be completed. She would prefer to have all the relevant facts at hand before making a decision. She does not rely on gut feeling, and is uncomfortable with taking risks. While this would probably serve her well in most instances, she would probably find it harder to make quick, aggressive decisions.

In her view, the supposed distinction between the potential of men and women as managers is overemphasised. She does not believe that gender has anything to do with the ability to handle work-related stress, and thinks that the common perception that women are too emotional to become good managers is a myth. She would reject the notion that in order to succeed in male-dominated organisation, a woman should behave like a man, but nor should she need to use her womanly charms. She feels that women have only to fight for their rights and strive to be more competent and work harder to keep pace with their male colleagues. She believes that in due course, people who are good at what they do, regardless of gender, will receive proper recognition.

I never really thought of strategising in my career. I just enjoyed what I have been doing and I believe that anything worth doing, is worth doing well. Then I just float into my current position, perhaps with a little dose of good luck. (female marketing manager)

This woman, who was employed in a large multinational company, did say, though, that the younger budding woman manager should strategise more, give her career path more thought, network more, and even choose the right type of husband as part of her strategy, to facilitate her success as a manager as well as wife and mother. In the AIM/LPPM study, one feature which distinguished women managers from their male counterparts was that hardly any of the respondents had consciously prepared their career strategies. It would be worth investigating whether my small interview study has revealed a shift in attitude over the last decade.

Conclusion

In spite of the male-dominated management scene in Indonesia, women managers have been increasingly making their mark, gradually gaining higher representation in management positions. But they are still a new breed, and their road to success is fraught with difficulties mainly imposed by traditional cultural value systems and a hierarchical class structure. Their own values are frequently a mixture between traditional and modern, resulting in inner conflicts.

The few women who have 'made it' mostly attributed their success to their own hard work and the support from boss or mentor and, most of all, husband. The role of women in the work force has become more and more important in Indonesia. The number of women in the labour force has now reached over 40 per cent, spread over almost all sectors of employment, and is expected to grow even further. This might be attributed to a variety of factors, including the Indonesian Constitution of 1945 which grants every Indonesian man and woman equal political rights, equal status and equal opportunities for employment; the existence of Indonesian Labour Laws and the existence for over a decade of a Minister for the Role of Women to ensure participation and provide support to women.

Unfortunately, such developments which look good in quantitative terms are not quite in line qualitatively. The majority of Indonesian women workers are in low income jobs. Although there are no legal constraints on women's employment, Indonesian women still suffer from various types of discrimination at work due mainly to the influence of traditional social attitudes and customs rooted in history and culture.

Notes

1. Which, in Indonesia, are published about two years later than the last year to which the data pertains.

2. Funded by the Canadian International Development Agency (CIDA), 300 respondents for each of the three categories, that is about 60 per country per category completed questionnaires; a 10 per cent sample was then selected for in-depth interviews.

3. I was in a unique position in relation to this survey. I was one of the respondents when working as a marketing manager in a multinational corporation and I was later involved in the study in Indonesia through my work in the Institute for Management Education and Development (LPPM), which is AIM's partner for the earlier studies. In an attempt to update the findings in 1996 I again interviewed 20 women managers, half of whom were from educational institutions, using the same AIM questionnaire. My findings were consistent with the previous studies.

4. *Editors' note*: The statistics provided by Chrysanti Hasibuan-Sedyono do not break down the type of work that these women were mainly employed to do. It is likely, in the Restaurant and Hotel sub-category at least, that the preponderance of women can be in part explained by the nature of the work, i.e. menial.

5. *Editors' note*: An interpretation by envious men! In fact as most women point out, biologically it is extremely unlikely for anyone to be menstruating and on maternity leave at the same time! Women are also less likely to put themselves in the position of annual pregnancies than men are to put them there, especially if pursuing their careers (the women that is).

6. *Editors' note*: In British Columbia, Canada, Jane Grzybowski in (1982) became the first woman crew member Coastguard Search and Rescue allowed to participate in full rescue activities on a Coastguard hovercraft. She insisted that she be tested criterion by criterion against the list of tasks a crew member be required to do. This approach has proved generally effective all over the world in debunking spurious physical incapacity arguments against women participating in traditionally male occupations. It should be noted that this tactic is most effective when occupational tasks are broken down into job specifications, as is required by most equal opportunities policies.

7. *Editors' note*: The chapter by Fiona Leach *Gender on the aid agenda: women, men and educational opportunity* provides a full discussion of this point.

8. In Indonesia, 'professor' is not a managerial position but a distinctive academic title. The title is given to only one or two people in each department, selected because of their excellent academic credentials the number of projects they have managed successfully is another criterion, thus 'professors' can undoubtedly be said to possess significant management skills.

9.   *Editors' note*: In this context the 'partners' referred to appear to be male: however, it is not unusual for an assumption of heterosexuality to prevail in, even to govern, workplace relations (see Mac an Ghaill, 1994).

10. *Editors' note*: this portrait of women managers does not tell us about women in management positions who need to work financially. Indeed the notion of workforce consisting of women managers deliberately and voluntarily keeping their salaries below those of their husbands has to be outside the concept of 'equal pay for equal work'. We are reminded of the middle-class and wealthy ladies carrying out 'good works' before the inception of the welfare state in Britain.

11. Of course this would have to be checked with the employees before asserting that this is what actually happened, but the point is this is what the managers believed they were doing.

References

Asian Institute of Management (AIM) (1987) Indonesia's Country Report, *A Country Profile on Women Managers in Business Organisations Project*, Manila.

Asian Institute of Management (AIM) Institut Pendidikan dan Pembinaan Manajemen (1989) Indonesia's Country Report, *A Country Profile on Women Managers in Non Profit Organisations and Women Entrepreneurs Project*. Manila.

Biro Pusat Statistik (Central Bureau of Statistics; CBS (1991)) bekerjasama dengan Kantor Menteri Negara Urusan Peranan Wanita (1991) Indikator Sosial Wanita Indonesia.

Biro Pusat Statistics (CBS, 1991-1995) *Labour Force Situation in Indonesia*.

Biro Pusat Statistics (CBS, 1996) *Population of Indonesia: Results of the 1995 Intecensal Population Survey*.

Darsa, M. and Rizal, Y. (1993) Manajer Wanita: Antara Persepsi dan Realita, *Eksekutif,* Mei: 60-66.

Ihromi, T.O. (1990) Wanita Bekerja Dimata Pria, makalah disampaikan dalam Seminar Hari Kartini oleh majalah Femina.

International Labour Organisation (1993) *A Comprehensive Women's Employment Strategy for Indonesia,* Final Report of an ILO/UNDP TSSI Mission, Bangkok: ILO Regional Office for Asia and the Pacific.

Mac an Ghaill, M. (1994) *The Making of Men: Masculinities, Sexualities and Schooling*. Open University Press.

Soekarsono E. (1994) 'Robby Djohan: Saya Tidak Ingin Ngoyo Lagi.' In Femina: No. 29/XXII.

Susanto, A. (1988) Wanita Karir dalam Pemerintahan, makalah disampaikan dalam seminar Dialog Pria-Wanita: Wanita dalam Manajemen, antara Citra, Fakta, Harapan, Jakarta.

Warta Ekonomi, V Wanita *Eksekutif* (1993) (4) Oktober 19: 35-38.

World Bank (1992) *Indonesian Women in Development: A Strategy for Continued Progress*. Internal Discussion Paper East Asia and the Pacific Regional Series. Report No. IDP-112. Washington DC World Bank.

Chapter 7

Good education management: women's experiences

Jeanette Morris

Introduction

In the Caribbean, education policy is not planned or managed by women despite and government policies to equalise educational opportunity in many of the territories. Drayton and Cole-Georges (1991, p.189) suggest that

> this under representation of women in decision making positions exists alongside an education system and a culture which perpetuates stereotypical views of male and female roles.

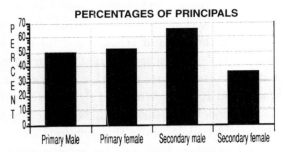

In Trinidad and Tobago 73.6 per cent of primary teachers and 56 per cent of secondary teachers i.e. the majority, are women. However this majority is not reflected at the level of principal, as can be seen from Figure 1. In 1995, the percentage of male and female primary heads was 49.16 per cent and 50.84 per cent respectively. At secondary level, proportions were 65 per cent and 35 per cent (Ministry of Education, 1995). In other words, at both primary and secondary level, male teachers, despite being proportionately fewer in number, are more likely to be promoted to senior levels in school management.

The existing dual secondary school system in Trinidad and Tobago is under review, and this complicates any attempt to survey current provision. Secondary schools are either state-owned or denominational, i.e. owned by the denomination but staffed by teachers who are public servants, paid by the state. In the old system, typically single sex denominational state-assisted schools offered seven-year routes to 16+ and Advanced level and also a five year route to 16+ examinations. This system is gradually being replaced by comprehensive schools for pupils from 12 to 16+ which are mixed sex, and which offer students the choice of an academic or a vocational route, particularly after age 14.

The total number of secondary schools is 100 of which 35 are headed by women. There are 46 schools in the traditional sector i.e. mainly single sex, both 5 and 7-year schools. Of these 22 have female principals. Seventeen are principals of seven-year schools, thirteen of which are denominational single-sex schools, and four co-educational schools. Five are principals of 5-year co-educational schools. In the new sector large co-educational schools institutions there are few female principals. In the junior secondary schools for 12 to 14 year olds, there are seven female principals out of 24. There are four female principals out of 16 in the senior secondary and comprehensive schools which have between 1,500 and 1,800 students and 100 teachers (Ministry of Education, 1995). The data show that in Trinidad and Tobago men are more likely than women to be secondary heads. The distribution of female principals within this varied system shows a clear pattern, that female heads in Trinidad and Tobago are more likely to be found in single-sex girls' schools and schools for younger pupils, rather than in co-educational schools for older adolescents. This pattern is similar to findings of cross-cultural research in high and low income countries (Davies, 1990, p. 62).

FEMALE PRINCIPALS BY SCHOOL TYPE

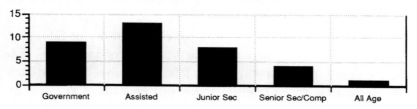

Reorganisation into mixed-sex comprehensive schools thus has implications for the career path of women teachers by effectively decreasing the likelihood of their gaining positions as principals.

The research reported in this chapter investigated 'successful' women, i.e. those currently in positions of senior management in schools, in order to ascertain:

- what routes women took in their access to management

- what motivated them to seek a management position

- whether they brought a particular concept of management or specific strategies to the exercise of management.

Data were collected from a questionnaire of all principals and vice-principals in Trinidad and Tobago and through interviews with seven women secondary heads. The interviews were recorded and transcribed, and from the individual accounts, patterns of career development and good management practice were discerned. Interview subjects represented all school types except the composite school. The two major ethnic groups in Trinidad and Tobago are Indo-Trinidadian and Afro-Trinidadian; both were included. One subject was a mixed Jamaican married to a Trinidadian. All the women were successful heads whose leadership qualities had been realised and encouraged by the administrators under whom they began their careers. Family responsibilities had not impeded their career development because they had spouses or extended family networks which provided support. They were well qualified and were representative of the so called 'intellectual elite', the result of policies of equal opportunity and national development of the post-independence Trinidad and Tobago. These policies provided free primary and secondary education for all and highly subsidised tertiary education to those who qualified. Under these conditions, women like these should have had no difficulty in gaining access to educational management. Their experiences therefore shed light on the processes that help or hinder women from access to management. In addition, in the multi-cultural context of Trinidad and Tobago the ethnic and cultural diversity of the respondents showed how cultural practices shape attitudes to women's roles.

Research perspectives

School management has traditionally been divided along gender lines, with men heading boys' and mixed schools and women typically heads of girls' schools. There has been a perception that the job of head needs certain traits and qualities generally associated with males:

> aggressive competitive behaviours, an emphasis on control rather than negotiation and collaboration and the pursuit of competition rather than shared problem-solving (Al-Khalifa, 1989, p.89).

This association of school leadership and masculinity has been reinforced by the imposition of 'an inappropriate business model of management on schools' (Court, 1994 p. 34) which has led to a transformation of school administration from a professional/collegial to a managerial/ bureaucratic model (Ball, 1990). The principal of a school is now compared to the chief executive of a company. Changes in school organisation, like the introduction of large comprehensives, have fuelled the need for better management in schools. The focus on management is also linked to the question of accountability as educa - tion costs escalate and state funding decreases. The managerial model however, coming as it does from organisational theory, has been criticised as male-centred. It assumes that findings can be generalised to both men and women (Shakeshaft, 1989; Alban-Metcalfe and West, 1991). This leads some women to question their suitability for management posts since they perceive that the qualities they possess and the management styles they espouse are not those normally cited in the literature on good management.

Research on whether men and women have different managerial styles has yielded mixed results. Most studies using survey methods have found no significant differences in administrative behaviour between male and female principals (Adkison, 1981, Davies and Gunawardena, 1992). A USA study which reviewed the research on gender and leadership style (Eagly, Karau and Johnson, 1992), found some evidence of gender differences. Female principals tended to adopt a more democratic and participative style than that of their male counterparts. Other qualitative studies (Shakeshaft, 1989; Rosener, 1990; Kelly, Hale and Burgess, 1991) also support the idea of management styles which are gender related. The argument has been advanced that any differences observed may be the result of women managers drawing upon the skills and attitudes developed from different life experiences (Court, 1994). Kelly suggests another possibility, which is that: 'men and women combine different behaviors in different ways to produce alternate impacts' (Kelly, 1991, p.108).

Good educational management needs to be seen not as a polarisation between perceived masculine and feminine leadership styles but as an integrated, holistic concept of management that allows for the incorporation of behaviours characterised as both masculine and feminine. Marshall's research on women managers (1984) suggests an integrated approach based on the principles of 'agency', i.e. achieving change through action and 'communion' which values interdependence. In this integrated approach managers both male and female can draw upon a repertoire of behaviours and choose the most appropriate for the particular school context. Since most research into management has used a male concept of management to document how women managers differ from men, there is need for research to move away from this focus to look instead at what women managers actually do on the job.

Educational Managers in Trinidad and Tobago

To place the interview data in context, a questionnaire was circulated to all principals, acting principals, vice-principals and acting vice-principals in secondary schools in Trinidad and Tobago. Eighty-one responses were received which represented a 43 per cent response. Of the managers who responded 38 were male, 42 were female and there was one response which did not specify gender. More than half the male respondents (i.e. 21) were actually principals at the time of the survey; so were ten of the women respondents. In contrast, at the entry level to school management, i.e. in the post of acting vice-principal, there were 16 women and only 6 men. As expected from Ministry of Education data, the majority of the female principals were in girls' schools. The male principals, however, were fairly evenly divided between co-educational and boys' schools. Half of the female principal respondents were single and more than half childless, which is interesting in so far as none of the male interview subjects were. Most of the principals were aged between 51 and 55 years, but on average the male principals were older than their female counterparts and had been principals longer.

However no inferences can be drawn from this evidence alone, as the response rate was not high enough to provide even the beginnings of a representative sample.

PRINCIPALS AND VICE PRINCIPALS BY GENDER

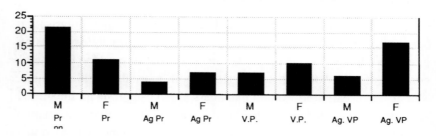

In Trinidad and Tobago principals are usually selected from practising vice-principals or from principals who desire a lateral move. Only in exceptional cases are classroom teachers promoted without having first served as vice-principal. From the survey data it appeared these rare cases usually occurred in the denominational schools, where other criteria for principalship e.g. religious persuasion, may overrule seniority claims.

Principals and vice-principals were asked how often they had applied for promotion before being successful. Among principals in the sample very few had actually applied for promotion. Although a formal selection procedure does exist – posts are advertised, application sent in, interviews held and persons appointed, an informal procedure seems to exist as well. Many principals indicated that they had been contacted and asked to apply for certain posts. However men in the sample tended to have made more applications than women. All the principals and vice-principals who responded had similar qualifications. The preponderance of men as principals suggests that men are more tenacious and likely to continue to apply for promotion, even following unsuccessful applications. It is also possible that, even when women are well qualified 'the self-perpetuating nature of the organisation, its ethos and structures still limit women's chances of promotion' (Adler, Laney and Packer, 1993, p.25). It is against this background therefore that women's experiences as managers and their concept of good educational management was explored.

Routes to management

In Trinidad and Tobago the route to management in educational institutions usually allows for teachers to gain practical experience of management prior to being put in charge of a school. The vice-principalship serves as a period of apprenticeship where, ideally, individuals work with the principal and are inducted into the tasks of management. If these persons have no formal training in management, they are usually sent to training courses given by the Ministry of Education, the University of the West Indies or the Teachers' Union (TTUTA).

Four of the women interviewed had taken postgraduate courses in administration at the University and found that this had helped them considerably.

> Having done the Ed. Admin. and all the theory and so on, you feel a lot more confident you feel, look the theory says so and so and the research has indicated so and so therefore you know you're not on the wrong track. (Mrs B)

> One thing I learned about was needs assessment. You know sometimes we hop in and try to change something without even doing a needs assessment. To me that was the most important thing I learnt, needs assessment and being a change agent. And I think if I had not done the Masters' programme, note I have not finished the Masters' programme, if I had not even done it I would not have been as successful as I was. (Mrs G)

Other women focused on the practical experience gained serving in a number of different capacities in the school.

> I used to be in almost every committee you can imagine – you know if we were having staff meeting and nobody would volunteer to take the notes I would take the notes, organise the graduation, sell material for the graduation dresses all these things. (Mrs L)

> So from early in my days at the school, they gave me a number of things, posts of responsibility... the school magazine, they put me to head that, to start the computer department, that was my job; the school library needed doing over they gave me a year to do over the whole library, set it on stream. (Mrs P)

Much of the practical preparation these women received was linked to their identification by their superiors as potential managers and being actively mentored towards assuming that role. One woman was identified and sent for training as part of a succession plan for the school:

> Actually when the previous administration decided that I should seriously consider applying for the post, the principal suggested that I do a course in administration that TTUTA was putting on. I had not even been aware of it, she signed me up for it and I took it. (Mrs J)

Good educational management in many cases is the cumulative result of a long period of apprenticeship and training. The questionnaire data suggest that women's participation in management training is growing because the majority of the respondents at the entry level management position of acting vice-principal are women. So unless existing constraints keep them excluded, more and more women should become visible in educational management. It is interesting to look at the reasons women themselves advance for seeking or deferring promotion.

What motivated the women to seek a management position?

All seven women interviewed were married with children. Three had not taken the initiative to seek promotion but had been encouraged to do so by their principals or school supervisors. Two of these rejected the idea when it was first suggested to them.

> Under Mr P (the principal) I did a lot of administrative work and a couple of circulars passed and he said you know I notice that you are not applying for any promotion for anything... he suggested it. (Mrs G)

> She (the principal) said, I see you in this chair one day. At the time I didn't take it seriously at all, just laughed and I said, I can't cope with my three little children how am I going to cope with seven hundred? (Mrs J)

However in time both women did accept the responsibility of administration and were very successful. The third woman acted on the suggestion of the school supervisor and got the promotion easily. At the time there was a massive expansion of the educational system and administrators were needed for the new schools. This provided the opportunity for some women to move into administration.

The move to a management position in a new sector school was not always the result of a desire to be an administrator. Mrs B, a teacher at a seven year girls' school, had other reasons for applying for a deputy principal's post in a new sector junior secondary school.

> I started thinking of it when I was getting a little tired of teaching exam classes, although they were successful classes, but I felt pressured and I felt that I wanted a break ... So the only other avenue for me was probably to move into a vice-principal's position because I really felt the need to shift away from teaching.

A heavy teaching workload was also the reason for Mrs L's desire to move into administration.

> One of the things that made me want to get out of teaching was all the SBA's (school based assessments) ad infinitum, SBA's, SBA's that was too stressful. (Mrs L)

The other two women came into administration through vacancies occurring in their schools; in one case as the most senior teacher she was made to act as vice-principal, and subsequently became principal. In the other case she applied for the post, encouraged by her husband:

> The post became vacant, I didn't intend to leave Newtown secondary and I thought I should apply for the vice-principal's post. It's there, I do administrative work... and I felt that I could do a good job... I think most of my encouragement comes from home. (Mrs P)

As managers, many of these women approached the task of educating their charges as if they were their own children.

> We wanted to make sure that it was the kind of school that if our children had to come to it we would be glad to have them there. (Mrs B)

> I believe if I am in a school it must be good enough for my children so my son is here at the moment. (Mrs L)

> I have always felt and I still do feel the most important duty is to the children. Teachers will come and teachers will go, the children must be treated properly. (Mrs E)

Most of these women were not strongly motivated to go into administration. They had to be encouraged and persuaded by mentors or husband that they were capable of doing the job. Others saw administration as a break from teaching. However once they were doing the job they were committed to ensuring that their students got the best possible experience and performed highly.

Concepts of management practices

From the interviews it was evident that most of the women favoured a collaborative management style. Emphasis was placed on team work, shared decision making, consultation and delegation of responsibility to teachers. Most felt that teachers needed to be brought into the decision-making process so that they could make a greater contribution. Mrs P put her views very clearly:

> I have an idea where I'm going but I'd like to feel everyone is on board. I tend to try to get around to that even if it takes a long, long time.

Another woman explained how she managed her school:

> I have a very open system, I meet frequently with the heads of my departments... We have lots of sub-committees even for things like social events in the school... so I delegate more and more to the department. (Mrs J)

Many principals saw themselves as part of a team with the vice-principals and teachers, working together for the good of the school. Mrs B spoke of her relationship as vice-principal with her principal in the junior secondary school and the fact that together they were a good management team, seen as such by the staff.

> We complemented each other. It worked well, it did not mean that we did not have a difference of opinion, but we were always united to the staff... the staff always saw us as one.

In two cases where brand new schools were established, teachers and administrators got together as a team before classes began to decide on goals and work out systems. Each principal as team leader had a vision for her school and felt that her leadership was important in bringing that vision to reality. Mrs. P. felt that her school had the potential to be a top school and tried to make that a shared goal.

> I set out first to sell them (the teachers) on the idea of what I called a magnet school. We must put in a programme that people would want to put us as first choice.

Her response to the community's perception of the school as a less desirable alternative to others outside of the district was to try to change that perception and through excellence achieve a reputation that would attract students not only of the community but from further afield. Another head's vision centred on improving the academic achievement of the pupils and enhancing the reputation of the school through scholarships won. Yet another, when sent to a school where discipline had deteriorated through absentee leadership, had a vision of an orderly school where teachers and children would be in their classes. For these principals the relationship with their staff was a key component of their management strategy.

> And again we thought if we could run a good outfit then we would get the morale high, and once the morale is high no one would want to be associated with a school that is breaking down. And so we went ahead and it really worked out, the teachers felt very good about themselves and the school. (Mrs B)

Another head had given permission for a graduate student to administer a questionnaire to teachers on the school's management. Feedback based on the results of the anonymous questionnaire was encouraging:

> Many of the teachers through that questionnaire you see they feel we are doing something, we are making a positive impact not just on the school but on the community, that their work is meaningful. (Mrs G)

Good staff morale was also seen to be a function of administrators who treated staff as individuals with personal as well as professional lives and showed concern for their well-being. This was achieved in some cases by putting systems in place to relieve teachers of clerical work by using computers for student records, or by delegating some disciplinary responsibility to senior students.

Concern for teachers' personal problems was also seen as necessary for a good relationship between administration and staff.

> We felt as administrators, one of the things we have discussed, that we must bend over backward to accommodate our teachers. Some one comes in frowning today, let's make it a habit, Miss how is your son, how is your daughter? Let us know something about them, right, because it's not always possible to leave the baggage by the gate. And we must be seen... that you make a difference to us we care about you. (Mrs G)

Friendly and cordial relations with staff were seen as a way of creating a climate of trust and cooperation. As Mrs L said: 'I love to meet with staff, I go and visit them where they are, I chat with them and that kind of thing'.

More than one principal referred to the' open door' policy which ensured that they were always available to anyone who needed to see them. Another strategy used by heads to increase teacher motivation and effectiveness and to lift the standard of the entire school, was professional development. One principal started by encouraging those teachers who were not yet professionally trained to obtain such training. Then she introduced the idea of clinical supervision, even for those already trained, where as principal she would visit classes to monitor teachers' delivery of the curriculum. She also introduced 'professional days' dedicated to staff development activities. To emphasise the importance of the professional aspect of teachers' work she changed the traditional order of business at staff meetings to deal with professional matters first, and routine matters last.

Similar strategies were used by principals to gain the support and cooperation of students and their parents. Concern for students' welfare, building their confidence and self-esteem and dealing with them as individuals all contributed to better motivation. Making the school an integral part of the community and enlisting community support for the school's efforts also proved to be successful.

Many perceptions of what constituted good management practice surfaced among interviewees. Some focused on organisational skills, the principal's ability to plan ahead, to set up systems and create a structure of management within the school. Others saw good interpersonal relations and effective communication as key. Still others recognised certain qualities which they thought helpful in the task of management:

a willingness to accept responsibility, the courage of one's convictions, patience and the ability to remain calm in a crisis. As the school principal now has to be plant manager, financial manager as well as instructional leader, more than one woman cited the ability to compartmentalise and to juggle many tasks at the same time as a crucial skill. These women were confident about their capabilities and the contribution that they could make as principals.

Several constraints were identified which hampered their ability to manage effectively, the most frequently cited being the lack of resources. This affected the size of the teaching and support staff as well as the provision and maintenance of plant and equipment. One principal indicated that the time she spent on fundraising and repairing the school undermined the quality of education offered as this time could better be spent monitoring teaching. Three of the women cited difficulties in management which arose from gender bias. All three managed schools in rural areas. In two cases Indo-Trinidadian men teachers, who came from a patriarchal culture and religious background, were unwilling to accept the authority of female principals, questioning their decisions and challenging them somtimes leading to unpleasant confrontations. In the third case an Afro-Trinidadian woman applied for the principal's position at a school in an isolated rural community which was largely Indo-Trinidadian. She was the most qualified candidate but was given the vice-principal's post instead as the selection committee felt that the community would object on grounds of gender and ethnicity. When she took up her post she found that the committee's assessment of the community's views was accurate and that in addition she was perceived as being on the wrong side of the political fence. All three principals weathered these difficulties successfully and in time earned the respect of the staff and community.

Bureaucratic procedures and a lack of flexibility by the Ministry of Education were also cited as serious constraints with Principals were also constrained by regulations which at times prevented creative solutions from being implemented. However they also cited avenues of support, for example networking with other principals and the help of parents and the community.

Conclusion

The individual experiences of these women managers raise key issues about women and management. Women's absence from management is not because they are any less qualified than their male counterparts. In many cases as well as equivalent qualifications, they have wider experience, especially in the area of interpersonal relations. A factor associated with success mentioned by several subjects is the encouragement of mentors and the support of families who encouraged the women to apply for senior posts. They were highly motivated with an overwhelming concern for the children in their charge and the desire to create a school climate in which excellence would flourish. Perhaps the most interesting aspect is their own descriptions of their management style — although of course further research would be required to ascertain whether these were the styles of management these women really did use. The school context itself is also a significant influence on the appropriateness of management style and how this is perceived. However, all the accounts stress collaboration, cooperation and good interpersonal relationships, particularly with teachers, as being crucial to the administrators' ability to manage effectively.[1] This suggests that the women managers in the sample resisted conformity to the traditional concepts of management and evolved their own style. Because of the small number of women interviewed this research can only indicate very tentative patterns and highlight some of the issues which need to be dealt with in future research. Their practice eschews a bureaucratic approach of close supervision and strict adherence to rules and regulations, and focuses on delegation, allowing teachers to develop their potential by accepting responsibility and sharing in decision-making. Home and family are not necessarily deterrents to women who wish to pursue careers in management: family factors affect women's decisions about school type and location when applying for management positions, but not to the exclusion of all other considerations. Management practice based on women's experiences brings to the concept of good management a whole new dimension which implies: 'a dialectical relation between our domestic experience of nurturing children and our public project to educate the next generation' (Grumet, 1988, p.5).

The skills and experiences of women managers are appropriate for today's schools. At present a minority, they should be recognised as full partners and given equal opportunities to play their part.

Note

1. *Editors' note*: this, as is pointed out by Venitha Soobrayan in her chapter in *Gender neutral leadership: a myth nurtured by leadership?* book is in direct contrast with old fashioned management handbooks still in use which stress the need for objectivity, distance and efficiency.

References

Adler, S., Laney, J. and Packer, M. (1993) *Managing Women*. Buckingham, Philadelphia: Open University Press.

Alban-Metcalfe, B. and West, M. (1991) 'Women Managers'. In J. Firth-Cozens and M. West (eds.) *Women at Work*. Milton Keynes: Open University Press.

Adkison, J. (1981) Women In School Administration: a review of the research. *Review of Educational Research*. Vol. 51 pp 311-343.

Al-Khalifa, E. (1989) 'Management by Halves: Women Teachers and School Management'. In DeLyon, H. and Widdowson Migniuolo, F. (eds.) *Women Teachers: Issues And Experiences*. pp 97-109. Milton Keynes: Open University Press.

Ball, S. (1990) 'Management As Moral Technology'. In Ball, S. (ed.) *Foucault and Education*. London: Routledge.

Court, M. (1994) Removing Macho Management: lessons from the field of education. *Gender, Work and Organisation*, Vol. 1 No. 1 pp 33-49.

Davies, L. (1990) *Equity and Efficiency: school management in an international context*. Lewes: Falmer Press.

Davies, L. and Gunawardena, C. (1992) *Women and Men in International Management: the challenge for transparency*. Paris: IIEP.

Drayton, K. and Cole-Georges, J. (1991) *The Access of Women to Planning and Decision Making in Education in Ten Commonwealth Caribbean Countries*. Paper prepared for UNESCO.

Eagly, A., Karau, S. and Johnson, B. (1992) Gender and Leadership Style among School Principals: a meta-analysis. In *Education Administration Quarterly*, Vol. 28, No. 1 pp 77-102.

Grumet, M. (1988) *Bitter Milk: women and teaching*. Amherst: University of Massachusetts Press.

Kelly, R. (1991) *The Gendered Economy*. Newbury Park: Sage Publications Inc.

Kelly, R., Hale, M. and Burgess, J. (1991) Gender and Managerial Leadership Styles: a comparison of Arizona Public Administrators. In *Women And Politics*, Vol. 11, No. 2.

Marshall, J. (1984) *Women Managers: Travellers in a male world*. Chichester: John Wiley and Sons.

Ministry of Education, Educational Planning Division for Trinidad and Tobago (1995). *List of public schools*. Unpublished raw data.

Rosener, J. (1990) Ways Women Lead. In *Harvard Business Review*, November-December. pp 119-125.

Shakeshaft, C. (1989) *Women in Educational Administration*. Newbury Park: Sage Publications Inc.

Chapter 8

Transgressions into educational management

Devarakshanam Betty Govinden

'we are each other's harvest,
we are each other's business,
we are each other's magnitude
and bond.'
(Gwendolyn Brooks)

Preamble

I began writing a paper on women and educational management (November, 1993) when, quite unexpectedly, I was nominated to be Dean of the Faculty of Education. I had been arguing that women should be given spaces in our institutions for administrative experience, to be able to transform structures...to criticise 'male models of management'... For women in general, for other women, but NOT for ME!

My immediate reaction to the nomination was a series of protestations: I was inexperienced; there are many senior persons 'above' me; I had never done this before; I did not know the RULES... I'm not a 'management person'... I prefer teaching, reading and writing to 'managing'... Why did I feel that it was a little like committing intellectual suicide?

I realised that many of the arguments I was using were directly related to the way management positions were presently carried out. I feared being evaluated by the very criteria that I myself had academically contested and dismissed as antiquated, untenable, 'technicist'. And I found I was being challenged by my own arguments, counter-arguments, rationalisations, and reservations.

I had to fight barriers created within me through years of socialisation, fear of facing a riot at home, fear of failure... fear of working within all those daunting university structures... I had to listen to other voices – from deep within myself and around me... voices of encouragement and reassurance...voices from far away, like that of bell hooks (1989), who says

> We must be willing to restore the spirit of risk – to be fast, wild, to be able to take hold, turn around, transform...

I was being called to launch out into the deep...in faith and courage... to be vulnerable... And I had to go back: I had to go forward...

The context

We continue to celebrate the miracle of the first democratic elections in South Africa in 1994, an event that heralded much hope for a new era of change and transformation in every sphere of our country's life. Universities have had to show the effects of this change from the apartheid educational system. One of the many contributions to this rebuilding has been the work of the National Commission on Higher Education (1996). Dealing with numerous problems – finance, student and staff politics, technical institutional management – the Commission has accomplished much in the reconstruction of our tertiary educational system. But I was disappointed to note a glaring absence of concern about the question of women in management in higher educational institutions.

The University of Durban-Westville, where I work, is referred to as a historically-black university (HBU). It began as an institution for persons of Indian origin, and has in recent years been 'opened' to all population groups. All our universities have programmes of trans-formation, and issues of governance are much talked about and struggled over. We are particularly concerned that students are incor-porated in all decision-making structures. There have been many expected changes in our educational structures in this period of tran-sition in schools and universities:

> Although other organisations are open and vulnerable to their environ-ments and to internal threats to their stability, schools find themselves

> increasingly in the midst of competing and often conflicting professional
> and community expectations for their performance. Greenfield (1995)

My work has made me conscious of the continuing challenges of educational management, of its multi-dimensional nature. In this chapter I reflect on a few critical issues in educational management with our peculiar 'situational imperatives' (Greenfield, 1995), and from a gendered perspective.

There has been a wide range of concerns that women have been reiterating (from Forward Looking Strategies – Nairobi 1985, to The Platform for Action – Beijing, 1995) in relation to women and education. These include access to all levels of education, curriculum, teacher training, adult education, literacy, counselling, and vocational education. To cite one example, on our own continent, we notice that of 340 million women, 40 per cent are illiterate.

'Emancipatory politics' calls for fundamental and critical analysis of discrimination against women in all spheres so that they can become agents of change and transformation. Issues of gender and management, with particular reference to educational institutions in South Africa and elsewhere, are part of wider discussion of discrimination against women at personal and structural levels (Klein, 1993). This subject touches larger concerns such as cultural norms and practices, societal perspectives as well as questions of power, ideology and language.

The strides that we have taken in South Africa in respect of women's status is well known. There is major progress in Government, where 25 per cent of parliamentarians are women. The Government of National Unity accepted the Beijing Platform for Action. Representatives from South Africa attended the UN Conference on Women for the first time as an official delegation. In December 1995, our Government ratified the UN Convention on the Elimination of all forms of Discrimination Against Women (CEDAW), which has published a Manifesto specifically calling for a 'gender-inclusive culture through education'. Among the principles enunciated in the Manifesto is that of non-discriminatory gender inclusion, and this is rightly seen as fundamental to the organisation, structure and content of education. In addition, the Ministry of

Education proposed the formation of a Gender Equity Task Team to advise the Department of Education on a range of crucial issues pertaining to gender and education, which include consideration of affirmative action strategies for increasing the representation of women in professional leadership and management.

More and More Women ...

More and more women are joining the workforce outside the home. Traditionally we thought of women's work at home as different from formal labour. Much has been written in recent years of women's unpaid, unrewarded labour.

There has been a growing number of women teachers in our schools, colleges and universities in the last decade. Statistics show that women may be found in increasing numbers in formal employment, in businesses and firms, as well as in education. Numbers of women in our Faculty of Education show a steady increase.

Fewer and Fewer Women ...

While more women are entering educational institutions both at student and staff level, there is still a glaring imbalance between men and women, and especially black women, employed to teach.

Cheryl de la Rey looked at the composition of staff at the University of Durban-Westville in the early 1990s. She showed that women are: *concentrated at the lower levels of the academic hierarchy*. She also analysed race and gender as interlocking:

> Of the total number of male academic and research staff, Indian men constitute 50 per cent, Whites 44 per cent, Africans 5 per cent and Coloureds 1 per cent. However, while Indian men are the largest group in absolute terms, most professors are white men. Similarly, 50 per cent of women academics and research staff are Indian; 43 per cent are White, 5 per cent African and 1 per cent Coloured (de la Rey, 1993).

We have no African woman professors and senior lecturers, and no black women at the senior management level. The figures at the University of Durban-Westville at the end of 1995 show that at the professor and associate-professor level there are 40 per cent Indian males, 45 per cent White males, 5 per cent African males, no African females, 2 per cent Indian females, 3 per cent White females. There are two women on the University Council, but there are no women at the senior management and Deanship level. Of the numerous administrative 'branches' (15) there are no women as heads or directors, and of the 26 university institutes, centres and units (including research and outreach), there were only two women directors (Advice Desk for Abused Women and the Language Laboratory) and in 1996, one of them, the director of the Language Laboratory, left.

What effect does this numbers-image, in terms of race and gender, actually have on our increasing African population of students? Research on the gender and ethnic composition of educational institutions in the US shows that demographic composition adversely affects the educational outcomes of female and minority students (Konrad and Pfeffer, 1991). One needs to estimate the effect of the ubiquitous marginalisation of black women in the academy in South Africa, and the effect on black students who are generally taught by whites in dominant positions, as is the case in many of our tertiary institutions.

Women teach and men manage

Against this background, further imbalance needs to be highlighted. At the 'management level' there is a disproportionate ratio of men to women in our institutions. Gender imbalance in teaching and management in educational institutions creates perceptions that are difficult to contest:

> The common assessment that women teach and men manage...still holds true, despite a multitude of strategies to rectify the gender imbalance in educational management (Greyvenstein and Westhuizen, 1992).

The education system is:

> generally structured like a traditional home: men run the schools and women nurture the learners (Weber, 1981).

Judith Glazer also points to the images that are projected by such imbalance:

It is generally acknowledged that teaching is a feminised profession; educational administration is not. Because these two fields constitute distinct polarities, they provide an excellent opportunity to analyse the differential impact of feminist scholarship on education generally and teaching and school administration specifically. A feminist critique of teaching and administration can have conceptual and methodological implications in shaping current efforts to reform education, to professionalise teaching, and to restructure the organisation and administration of schools. (Glazer, 1991)

Lael Bethlehem (1992), writing at a national level here, draws attention to:

university policies and conditions of service; differential teaching and administrative loads; sexism and university culture, and the relationship between women's careers and their domestic/childcare labour.

Many argue that if women expect to be treated equally they should accept demands and conditions related to work and service that are in existence. But this often means that male-dominated structures and values are in place, and women have to cope with this background, having to work doubly hard for merit awards and promotions. Women still have to contend with a patriarchal culture that cuts across the family and community.

Feminists have argued that a 'paradigm shift' will include challenging the division between public and private worlds. The oft-used feminist slogan, 'the personal is political' may well be extended to 'the personal is professional'. While more women have to be recruited into educational institutions, with that should come a radical change in organisational ethos and structures, so that the reality of women's experiences is accommodated, or challenged and changed...

Living with contradiction

Most women in management positions (I use the term 'management' in the light of its widespread usage; but we need to reconceptualise, redefine, and re-interpret the field) have to juggle different and often competing roles of authority and subordination. My own role is not uniform or static, but complex, even contradictory. There are times when I reproduce the very roles I criticise, and there are times when I resist the stereotypical roles that I am expected to conform to. Negotiating between expected behaviour at home, in the community, and in the work situation often makes me conscious of the contradictions that I have to live with. Women also have to become skillful negotiators at our institutions, as we read the situations of conflict in various ways. There are several centres of authority on our campuses – students, staff, workers, management – to name the main ones. In times of conflict managers may be caught up in 'constituency wars' that develop.

As Dean I had wondered if persons around me expected me to conform to patterns of management that went before me, patterns set by male managers. I got the impression that if I did not seem to be performing as efficiently as they thought my predecessors had done, it was because they saw me as 'a mere woman'. When I delegated duties, my progressive colleagues saw this as a way of sharing or flattening the Deanship; I was sensitive, though, lest my conservative colleagues would see this as a dereliction of duty. For me as Dean, having constantly to prove myself was the most tempting and demanding part of being in a management role. Lurking in all this seemed to be double standards. Why was less demanded of male managers? Why was so much glossed over, or excused, when male managers were at the helm?

A psychology of work

Cassell and Walsh (1993), drawing from psychology, make crucial observations in relation to employment and gender issues. They categorise the barriers in organisational cultures. They stress the psychological barriers associated with taking on more powerful roles and outline some of the difficulties women face at the workplace. They suggest that psychology:

> needs to understand ways in which gender determines work organisation, particularly the links between gender, power and organisational culture. (Cassel and Walsh, 1993)

Using the concept of 'psychology of work' they describe and explain some of the covert, psychological barriers that prevent women from achieving positions of power in organisations. Women themselves have testified to the fact that they feel excluded, invisible, misunderstood, ignored and generally less powerful than men. Ferreting out why this is so is the beginning of change. We need to analyse the extent to which male-oriented perspectives underlie the practices and values of institutions and, crucially, the way that organisational analysis has been 'malestream'.

Psychological barriers at work are often difficult to describe and assess, but they work in powerful ways in the evaluation and assessment of staff. Appointment of staff, for example, is usually based on the rules of the game that are already in place. During the selection process for the Vice-Rector at our university a few years ago an attempt was made to include staff as participants. We heard speeches by prospective candidates (men who had 'made it' to the short-listed stage). They spoke of their 'vision for the university', and they answered questions from the floor. However, while this was an improvement on past closed selection procedures, it was still impersonal and interrogative interactive and dialogical. I wondered whether it might not have been more helpful to have interacted informally with all prospective candidates over a longer period.

A question of space – gendered locales

It is worth considering how differential power patterns in our educational institutions are reflected in spatial patterns. This is often accepted as part of the culture of educational institutions, but an analysis of the gendered nature of space, for example, reveals many inequalities (see Shilling, 1991).

At a simple level, we just have to look at the space for secretaries, usually female, in relation to their 'bosses', usually male; or that for junior staff v. senior staff, both academic and 'non-academic'. Class also plays an important role. Cleaning staff, for example, occupy small spaces, hardly creating an atmosphere for relaxation, compared to those provided for academic, administrative and technical staff.

We need a rigorous analysis of the role of space in institutional life, so that we do not assume that traditional environments, reflecting existing hierarchical patterns, are immutable.

Dealing with conflict

On our campuses our main need is for institutional stability. Our academic life is quite unpredictable, with conflicts of all kinds ready to flare up at any time. We feel the pressure to keep our campuses peaceful, as we are gravely concerned about the effect that student boycotts, strikes and marches and trashing of campuses has on the completion of academic programmes and the maintenance of good academic standards.

We are concerned, too, about the negative impact boycotts would have on the employability of our graduates, and on our funders and sponsors, both present and potential. We are sometimes forced to become media vigilantes, as we try to keep stories out of the newspapers. There is competition between our campuses about who has had a comparatively peaceful year. Much energy is expended in preventing campuses from becoming volatile; and this proceeds alongside necessary day-to-day organisation. There is also the inevitable conflict within faculties that one has to contend with. And in all this administrators are particularly vulnerable to the feeling of entrapment as well as of accountability.

It is worth noting that my male colleagues see it as a matter of personal pride that they do not 'take their problems home', whereas I tend to agonise long into the night. I reflect interminably on particular problems, trying to look at them from various vantage points. I am sensitive to criticism that I might not be acting decisively because I am a woman. Yet, when male managers are criticised for being indecisive, this is not attributed to the fact that they are male.

Management is being criticised for being in a state of 'paralysis' and 'rigor mortis'! I am tempted to measure my success as manager by my not collapsing under the strain or harbouring deep psychological wounds. It is sad when succeeding in an administrative office becomes equated in this way with survivalism.

Managers are overwhelmed by the difficulty of wading through competing claims in many situations of conflict. The work of 'top administrators' in South African universities has been described as being among the 'toughest jobs in the country' (*Mail and Guardian*: May 1996). Indeed administrators spend an enormous amount of time and energy dealing with conflict in various forms. There is despair that 'they spend their time fighting the same old fires on campus instead of implementing plans to turn their universities into world-class institutions' (*Mail and Guardian*: May 1996). The irony is that, in spite of the male senior managers being so heavily criticised, the perception persists that these 'tough' jobs are best handled by men.

I believe that one needs to be open to criticism, and resist either flagellating or vindicating oneself. What is crucial is the kind of support that is extended to managers, whether this advice, censure, affirmation, firm warnings of the danger signals for future conflagration, or just help with some of the administrative chores. Means to deal with conflict communally, where all the different constituencies work towards creative resolution, must be sought. What is particularly difficult to unravel on our campuses, ironically in a post-negotiation period, is the extent to which there are swings of the party political pendulum, and there is a need to be aware whether the ostensible, and often justifiable causes of conflict, are being fanned by alignments and disaffections of all sorts. Certainly the accusation of 'hidden agendas' is constantly heard by all contending groups against their adversaries.

There are many ways of dealing with change, and these demand institutional transformation. Negotiating roles in a participative rather than managerial (Hargreaves, 1994) way is fraught with obstacles as there are no set rules or stable expectations. David Hargreaves, argues that:

> In the new professionalism management and leadership are not people but functions that the school has to attend to by giving everybody, from principal to the most junior colleague, regular opportunities for leadership and management according to the nature of the problem, the circumstances at the time, and the available talent. (Hargreaves:1994)

The question of entryism
Davies makes the important point that the current conception of educational management encourages a notion of 'entryism', not on changing the structures and models of management.

It might be ... important to use gender analysis to analyse critically the derivations and implications of some of our ideologies about managerial or leadership styles, and to highlight how a feminist view might lead to a somewhat altered view of the practice of administration. (Davies, 1990, p. 74)

At our university two years ago we had a 'Search Committee' for a new Vice-Chancellor. There were no women on the committee. And no women seemed to have applied. Yet our university has a clearly stated policy that it is a non-discriminatory employer (Peacock, 1993, p.5). It was worth noting that no-one from the present (male) management group applied for the post. While there are grave difficulties for both men and women in these key higher education posts, the difficulties that women face loom larger. Among men it is usually an individual decision to stand for selection but women as a group are marginalised.

Lisa Ehrich (1994, p.11) draws attention to the lack of a mentoring programme for women, and emphasises the informal mentoring programme that men enjoy. She points out that male mentors tend to sponsor male protégés, and that one may see this as a kind of 'gender capital' working in favour of men. Ehrich points out that there is both explicit and implicit mentoring at institutional level. These categories draw attention to the awards, and direct and indirect opportunities that men are given to gain expertise in this field. Women should be given opportunities for administrative and organisational tasks in the same way as men. We should also become more aware of the tacit exclusion of women from informal socialising networks, where sharing of information takes place.

Re-defining the management terrain

I believe that 'entry' is not just about admittance to the hallowed spaces of power. It is also about questioning the way management is defined and executed.

There are only two women vice-chancellors at South African universities, one black and the other white. One, Mamphela Ramphele, Vice-Chancellor of the University of Cape Town (UCT) makes the important point that:

The creation of greater equity in higher education, and indeed in all areas of our inequitable society, has to involve three thrusts: greater access, opportunities for personal development, and a change in institutional culture (Ramphele, 1995, p. 207).

The under-representation of women has several consequences for our educational institutions. One important effect is how the management terrain is defined and redefined when women do not constitute a 'critical mass', either numerically or structurally.

Institutional cultures reflect the collective and cumulative customs, rituals, symbols and preferences of the people flowing through them over time. It is not surprising that most institutions in South Africa, including UCT, have a dominant white male culture...The problem is not the existence of the culture but the need to acknowledge it, examine it and change aspects of it that prevent its members from realising their full potential. (Ramphele, 1995, p. 208)

Ramphele (p. 208) argues that blacks or women have been seen as 'outsiders' in the broader society, and are therefore 'not well placed to negotiate the mystique of institutions in which they find themselves'. The challenge to educational leaders in our institutions is to become those 'transgressives', to use Ramphele's phrase, who will radically re-define the terms in which management takes place, and women have a particular contribution to make. The question is whether our campuses will be sufficiently nurturing environments for such 'trangressions'?

Bureaucrat, functionary, manager, academic, intellectual or transgressive?

Transgressions into educational management and re-defining this terrain, clearly means contesting the discourse and its implications. In this debate what is neglected is the place of the intellectual in our society. There is much need in South Africa for the intellectual, one who will reflect critically on the many perplexing contemporary questions. Intellectuals, of course, could come from any sector of life. In South Africa, historically, many have not been nurtured in the traditionally conservative academy. We are familiar with the vital role of these people, not merely in academia. We have also developed a necessary scepticism towards the division between university and the rest of society. Though not exclusive, there are developments in the last decade that have resulted in heads of our tertiary institutions, particularly black ones, comprising the leadership sector of our society.

Often senior managers in our educational institutions are looked upon as spokespersons on societal issues. But they need to articulate more critically and creatively. Giroux has called for 'writing the space of the public intellectual' (Olson and Hirsch, 1995, p.195). An important attribute of the intellectual is to claim the freedom and courage to express convictions, and to enable adversaries to do the same. Stanley Aronowitz calls for public spaces that reject the idea of a single narrative, so presenting politics as both molecular and multiple, transgressive and collective (ibid).

This does not mean that intellectuals work best when they are in some transcendental, autonomous role. Foucault has criticised these 'universal' intellectuals who pose as the 'intellectual conscience' of an age (Sarup, 1993, p.75), but are actually located in highly specialised and very narrow positions. We need to see intellectuals as set amidst the multiple and competing and contradictory discourses, and attempting to articulate their positions in the context of a 'micro-politics of localised struggles and specific power relations'

The communities we build on our campuses will be diverse and conflicting. But this does not mean that we cannot express our differences. Edward Said has stated, with moving simplicity:

> We are not obliged to break bread together, though that is always comforting. But to work together, what it takes is a deep, enduring respect based on an acceptance of our mutual humanities. (Said, 1996)

This is not to claim 'academic freedom' in some vacuous and glib way, and in the process simplify the causes of conflict, often moral, ethical and material. Many of our country's larger conflicts and tensions invariably find themselves in the campus crucible. The challenge for continuing redress of the inequities of the past requires us, men and women, to ensure that higher education becomes the resource it should be for the reconstruction and development of South Africa.

We need to nurture a different kind of ethic, where intellectual, critical thinking is not a narrow, rationalist contest, but connotes a 'complementarity of emotion and reason' (Phelan and Garrison, 1994). This makes room for contradiction and ambivalence in our daily responses to conflicts. Feminists have developed the notion of connected knowing, identifying with both sides of the controversies that plague us. This will help us to articulate the issues that divide us with greater empathy and compassion and allow for the free exploration of views that may be contrary to those acceptable to whoever may have the balance of power at the time. Women managers have an important role to play in this transformation.

References

Bethlehem, L. (1992) Gender, Affirmative Action and the composition of academic staff at South African Universities. Paper presented at UDUSA (Union of Democratic Universities Staff Associations) National Conference, 1992.

Cassell, C. and Walsh, S. (1993) Being Seen But Not Heard: Barriers To Women's Equality In The Workplace. The Psychologist, Vol. 6, No. 3, March 1993, pp110-113.

Davies, L. (1990) Equity and Efficiency? School Management in an International Context. Lewes: Falmer Press.

de la Rey, C. (1993). Are we a 'Non-sexist' university? In COMSA NEWS (Combined Staff Association), University of Durban-Westville, Vol. 6, No. 2, June 1993.

Ehrich, L.C. (1994) A Mentoring Programme for Women Educators. In School Organisation, Vol. 14, No.1, 1994.

Glazer, J. (1991) Feminism and Professionalism in Teaching and Educational Administration. Educational Administration Quarterly, Vol. 27, No. 3, August 1991, pp 321-342.

Greyvenstein, L.A. and van der Westhuizen, P.C. (1992) South African Women in Educational Management : an holistic approach. South African Journal of Higher Education. Vol. 12, No. 3, August 1992. pp.270-275.

Greenfield, W.D. (1995) Toward a Theory of School Administration: The Centrality of Leadership. Educational Administration Quarterly, Vol. 31, No. 1, February 1995. pp 61-86.

Hargreaves, D.H. (1994) The New Professionalism : The Synthesis of Professional and Institutional Development. Teaching and Teacher Education, Vol. 10, No. 4. pp 423-438.

hooks, b. (1989) Talking Back: thinking feminist, thinking black. London: Sheba.

Klein, G. (1993) Education Towards Race Equality. London: Cassell.

Konrad, A.M. and Pfeffer, J. (1991) Understanding the Hiring of Women and Minorities in Educational Institutions. Sociology of Education, Vol. 64, July 1991. pp 141-157.

Mail and Guardian, article entitled 'Harbinger of Hope for Campuses'. May 3-9 1996, p. 23.

National Commission on Higher Education (NCHE) (1996) Discussion Document. April, 1996, Pretoria.

Olson, G.A. and Hirsch, E. (eds.) (1995). Women Writing Culture. New York: Suny.

Peacock, K.S. (1993). *South African Universities: Race and Gender Factors in Employment Patterns.* Research commissioned by Union of Democratic Staff Associations (UDUSA), Johannesburg.

Phelan, A.M. and J.W. Garrison. (1994). Toward a Gender-Sensitive Ideal of Critical Thinking : A Feminist Poetic. In *Curriculum Inquiry*, Vol. 24, No. 3 (1994), The Ontario Institute for Studies in Education.

Ramphele, M. (1995). *A Life.* Cape Town and Johannesburg: David Philip.

Said, E. (1996). *Representations of the Intellectual.* New York: Vintage Books.

Sarup, M. (1993). *An Introductory Guide to Post-Structuralism and Postmodernism.* Athens, US: University of Georgia Press.

Shilling, C. (1991). Gender Inequalities and Educational Differentiation. In *British Journal of Education*, Vol. 12, No.1, pp 23-44.

Weber, M.B. et al. (1981). Why Women are Under-represented in Educational Administration. In *Educational Leadership*, January 1981, p 320.

Chapter 9

Conclusion

Eve's work is hard work even for Eve

Pat Drake and Patricia Owen

In this volume the authors have discussed a wide-ranging set of issues relating to professional women and their work. The fact that the workplace is an educational one means that the writers have had to consider themselves as a part of a system which deliberately sets out to inculcate the values of society to other, usually younger, people, in particular girls, whilst simultaneously being shaped by those values themselves. The analysis is enriched by the international dimension, especially the focus on developing and rapidly changing countries. In such countries legacies of colonialism, of apartheid, of transplanted, imposed cultures and values, have almost always bequeathed a heavy burden.

So the challenge for the contributors has been to scrutinise education itself, to examine the extent to which education *per se*, as well as women's participation in the management of it, is justified as a means of what could be seen as interference in the culture and traditions of other countries. This is a difficult thing to do – far easier to explain resistance to education in terms of ignorance or self-centred adherence to old and out-dated ways of life. Few would deny that children should have access to schooling, yet as several of the contributors show, (e.g. Lynn Davies and Zeeshan H. Rahman), things can look rather different when schooling itself and the infrastructure which provides it is held up for examination.

Several questions remain unanswered, for which we make no apology, given the genesis of the book, and it is worth clarifying the distinction between women's issues and gender issues. Women's issues are those which relate to women specifically because of their sex. Gender issues are a consequence of the feminisation or masculinisation of certain activities. Thus, maternity or menstruation leave are women's issues, whereas the provision of child care becomes a gender issue when it is put exclusively under the provenance of women. A gender issue for men would result from an expectation of providing all the financial support for the family. Gender issues can lead to stereotyping and there has been evidence (see Chrysanti Hasibuan-Sedyono) that this occurs to the detriment of women's progress in the workplace.

The theme of gender has served several purposes. Firstly, it has provided a context for educated professional women from both the developing and the developed world to discuss and then write about their observations and experiences. As with many aspects of women's lives, relating to issues of 'gender', a need to probe and understand the workings of generally male-constructed, and often male-dominated hierarchies and systems is international: common to women across the world – a need to develop an understanding of the system in which they find themselves. Some of the contributors to this book have written for the first time and as editors we are proud to have enabled this. Secondly, attention to issues of gender is currently important to the educational policies of developing countries. Thirdly, publicity, even when hostile, given to the politics of gender and equal opportunity, has enabled millions of women to gain insight and then improve their lives, both personally and professionally. The more discussion the better it is to raise issues related to social and cultural constructions and representations of what it means to be female and what it means to be male.

Above all, this volume provides a forum for an airing of work about the gendered nature of the school, the education of girls, the career patterns of teachers, the situation of women in education management, inequities between the work styles, prioritisations, decision making, of male and female managers. Men and women have to monitor and check how others may be faring, and to draw to public attention issues of inequity, unfairness or downright oppression.

The authors of chapters in this book may or may not wish to refer to themselves as 'feminists', and maybe the use of the term depends on how, pragmatically, these writers and practitioners wish to present their case within particular contexts. Nevertheless, there is no doubt that feminism, or at least perceptions of feminism, provides the structure and fuels the arguments these chapters present. This is a creditable stand on the part of all involved, as women in high status positions are often accused of turning their backs on women's issues. To be clearly identified as a feminist in the workplace is likely to be seen as saying good-bye to any prospect of promotion. Rude things are said about women who push women's issues at work and they can be conveniently marginalised as embittered, strange, 'other'. So analysis of power relationships is typically done by academics, often for consumption on Women's Studies courses in universities, (generally northern or western), one of the few types of workplace in which it may be considered relatively respectable for women to get together in groups, although again not totally without disadvantage (Morley and Walsh, 1995). That this book is able to put forward perspectives on management by women in managerial roles shows that the mass of voices prepared to speak out is growing, and that what is said is not just criticism from the marginal territory inhabited by the excluded, but is representative of the reality of being successful and female and maybe also black.

When stereotyping occurs, men and women are easily drawn into accepting responsibility for solving problems which are not their individual fault, but are structural in origin. For example, women do seem to experience dilemmas in terms of balancing home and work, and child care seems to be a perennial problem. In the developed world, child care is expensive; in developing countries it is cheap, but exploitative of less fortunate or less well educated family members or workers. In this discourse it is easy to look to the needs of the family as setting up obstacles to individual achievement, and diverting attention from the institutions themselves whose organisational practices quite likely do not acknowledge the day-to-day lives of the people who work in them (see Lynn Davies' chapter).

A further challenge offered by the book is to the friendliness of education as a working environment for women. We have seen that despite women's vast array of qualifications, they are not represented at the higher levels in the education system in the proportions that their academic credentials would suggest they should be. This applies at policy level (see Venitha Soobrayan's chapter), in universities (see Betty Govinden's and Chrysanti Hasibuan-Sedyono's chapters), in schools (see Jeanette Morris' chapter); there are hints too that classrooms are not women-friendly (see Jeanette Morris', Zeeshan H. Rahman's and Fiona Leach's chapters). It would appear that women are most accept-able in the education workplace only if they remain within their 'proper' sphere – with the youngest children, in the lower grade jobs, at elementary, not advanced levels, learning and teaching 'non-advanced subjects'. And as any teacher who is also a parent knows only too well, the organisation of school life makes it very difficult to participate fully in the schooling of one's own children, especially at elementary level when school events tend to be during the middle of the day. Of course this also applies to working parents generally; the point here is that parents who are teachers are quite unable to rearrange their professional schedules to participate in activities which relate to their own children, because they are involved in those same activities for the children of others.

In multiracial societies such as South Africa or the West Indies or Indonesia, respect for cultural values of ethnic groups other than one's own is currently a *sine qua non* of civilised behaviour. Yet appalling behaviour by men towards women is explained or even condoned on the grounds that traditions or cultural values are different. Jeanette Morris specifically draws our attention to this issue through her research. Anecdotal evidence also abounds[1], and it is high time that the 'problem' some men have in dealing with women as authority figures is resolved, not left to individual women to deal with in response to what may be outrageous rudeness or hostility.

Parallels spring to mind of the fight in the Anglican church for recog-nition of women priests. Eventually sense prevailed. Now that homo-sexuals are pressing to be allowed to prepare for the priesthood, exactly the same arguments are being rehearsed against this proposal. So it is not what the women or the homosexuals are in themselves which poses the threat, it is the group who will have to adapt to accommodate them who have the problem. This is not new, and it is particularly deep-rooted in the field of education. Caste or class background has also for long caused similar polarisation and resistance (Widdowson, 1983).

Western scholars (Goodson, 1992, Acker, 1989, Mac an Ghaill, 1994) have discussed the gendering of the educational institution in terms which differentiate between gender, sexuality, power and institutional access. In this context it is alarming to consider that the issues the contributors to this book characterise optimistically as 'unfairness', as obstacles to be overcome, are in fact endemic to an ideology of male supremacy and as such invisible to the perpetrators of this structure. Kathleen Casey (1993) has written about professionally qualified black women teachers being grateful for jobs as school cleaners and secretaries as late as 1960 in the USA. Despite perfectly acceptable qualifications, without a 'sponsor' they were unable to take up the posts for which they had been trained. The growth of equal opportunities legislation should have meant that such situations would never exist again, yet there is a strong sense of history repeating itself. In this light it is with a sense of foreboding that we see today the need for a 'mentor' for women to make the seniority of management. What happens to the resistors, to those individuals who challenge the status quo by virtue of some 'unacceptable' aspect of their being – be this their ethnicity, culture, class, sexual orientation or gender?

'Education' does not exist in a vacuum as an unproblematic 'good thing', untainted by the societies in which it exists. It is certainly not an 'absolute' good. It is in pursuing this theme that we face the real challenge of the hegemony of education as an international commodity which can be unproblematically and successfully transplanted into different cultures and contexts. As we have seen, many of the issues arising out of the accounts of the contributors are not new. Many of them are generating new forms of reaction; of moving forward. True, World Bank initiatives are encouraging girls to stay in school, but perceived hidden agendas related to this are now challenged. As Farida Akter, working at a non-governmental organisation in Dhaka, puts it:

> The World Bank doesn't have any development perspective on women, it just sees them as a means of reducing fertility rates. That is why they

educate girls; that is why mothers' clubs and co-operatives are encouraged. It even insists that girls have to drop out of the scholarship programme if they get married. (Akter, quoted in Kelly, 1994)

When initiatives for extending female education meet with success, and girls do come into schools, they can often end up in an even worse position than before. As a result, they may subsequently be seen as 'unable to cope'. Such a scenario is only too frequent, as we recognise similarities with women being blamed for male behaviour in for example the experience of Malawi schoolgirls (Kadzamira and Hyde, 1994), where girls attending secondary school, the very site of supposed educational freedom, are subject to risk of pregnancy and rape from fellow students and teachers. This argument is then used by parents and guardians to prevent their daughters from attending school, and who can blame them for trying to keep their girls safe?

But there are challenges to such a view, and encouragement can be taken from the outraged reactions of women to such incidents. A report in *The Asian Age* newspaper from Cuttack district in the impoverished Indian state of Orissa describes how, when a little girl was molested by her headmaster, an attack only discovered when the child refused to go to school the next day, '...a group of women armed with broomsticks and chappals (sandals)... assaulted the teacher'. The account concludes with the news that:

> The incident has sparked strong resentment among several women's organisations who demanded immediate formation of a Child Rights Commission in the state. (Mishra in Asian Age, 8 April 1997)

The questions should also be asked: why are careers in education somehow devalued when women take them up? Why is it a 'problem' if teaching is seen to be dominated by women? Why does the presence of a large number of women within a profession seem to devalue it?

> No country should pride itself on its educational system if the teaching profession has become predominantly a world of women. (Langeveld, 1963)

The direction of government policy in many parts of the world has been towards greater decentralisation and increased institutional autonomy. It is demonstrated in these chapters that getting girls into school and keep-ing them there is now seen as a vital adjunct to any programme of aid; to be viable and successful, even to get off the drawing board and see the light of day at all, any new 'development' initiative now has to make more than just a cursory nod at the 'gender agenda'. In fact there is now almost universal agreement that the key to sustained improvement and prosperity in the health, literacy and economic success (and reduced birth-rate) of families, villages, towns, cities... in fact whole nations, is the provision and support of education for girls.

Thus girls should and must have access to schooling as should women to teaching and to other careers in exactly the same way as their brothers. Yet as several of the contributions to this book show, it isn't quite as simple as that. The benefits of education in perhaps opening up possibilities for women to achieve a degree of financial independence, to move away from home, live alone, not marry, not have children, single-mindedly pursue careers, and to *take control* over their own lives are seldom discussed. It must here be borne in mind that using education as a lever with which to gain different life chances and expec-tations is something that only a very tiny percentage of the female school population are likely to do, or even to consider. But the possi-bilities are there, although they may never be overtly acknowledged, and with them the possibilities for education to act as a force which can transform girls' and women's lives on so many levels.

As Zeeshan H. Rahman describes, the benefits of education above all to the home and family of the little girl heroine are emphasised in the *Meena* stories. In one episode of this widely acclaimed cartoon series the story focuses on the day-to-day activities of a child who badly wants to attend school, but has first to prove its worth as an investment to her home, family and village, which she does triumphantly. Education is portrayed here as valuable in the benefits it brings not only to the girl herself, but above all to the family and the wider village community.

Interestingly, *Meena's* impact is not confined to the so-called develop-ing world, but has also been noted as giving a positive identity and 'permission to speak' to quiet, previously unforthcoming girls in some British schools (Newmark, *Times Educational Supplement, 28th February 1997*). Even when they *are* in school, girls can be marginalised, ghettoised, perceived as a 'problem.' Rarely, so it seems, is the achievement of girls noted as being as worthy of celebration. Throughout the world a challenge needs to be mounted to the view that it's all right for girls to be in school and their mothers and older sisters to be in education, as teachers or maybe even administrators and government officials – but only up to a point, so long as it doesn't go too far. The chapters in this volume issue such a challenge.

In every chapter, the writers have drawn our attention to things which are wrong in the field of education and of education management. Across the globe, so it seems, there is much in common to deplore. And yet strategies and tactics for remedy are suggested throughout; analysis and action is the key, not foundering in lament. Such energy has been reflected in the alacrity and enthusiasm with which contributors responded to our – probably unreasonable – demands as editors for changes, clarification, and all the other detailed minutiae attendant on producing a volume of this kind.

As we relate in our introduction, most of the women involved in the production of this book had met earlier, in the context of the British Council's 1995 Seminar. They wrote alone, but with the insights and questions raised by those earlier mutual debates undoubtedly in mind. Indeed in some instances, (for example in Venitha Soobrayan's chapter), it was this discussion and interaction with fellow delegates which sparked off the ideas now crystallised in this book. The editors also found that shared ideas and argument shaped its pattern.

The title of this concluding section to our book is a quote from work by a group of women principals in the US, who met and kept diaries which they shared with each other to analyse, and also to provide mutual support. One of the group, Joanruth Hirshman wrote in her journal:

> The sum of all these life experiences causes me to reflect. I was the sole carer for my grandmother, my mother and my father. I shared responsibility for my mother-in-law and my father-in-law [.......]. Were all these experiences, feelings and insights my true training for the principalship? Organising, managing and distributing time and resources were lessons learned [...].

The warp to the woof were the emotions, feelings and realisations. I learned from my deepest depths about how insensitive individuals behave towards the helpless. I need, I want to personalise the institution called school. Human beings have a right to be treated with respect and dignity. [...] Eve's work is hard work, even for Eve. (Christman *et al*, 1995)

It is respect for human beings which has underlined all the contributions and suggestions which the authors believe would make education better. It is unlikely that women will shed their multiple activities, or delegate them. What we hope is that women are moving towards understanding themselves as agents of change in the educational environment, that having climbed into the ivory tower, they are able to see clearly how the place can be improved or even rebuilt, and to be instrumental in that reconstruction. This generates more work, more commitment, more responsibility. Eve's work is indeed hard work, even for Eve.

Note

1. For example, I (PD) was one of two women amongst a party of six visiting a teachers' college As soon as the woman principal of the college had left her office to fetch drinks for the visitors, the male professor of education said to one of the other men 'I wouldn't work for a woman, would you?'. When I indicated that I had noted the comment, the professor continued to talk in local language. I wouldn't have understood, except that the words 'Margaret' and 'Thatcher' are not translatable!.

References

Acker, S ed. (1989) *Teachers, Gender and Careers*. Lewes: Falmer Press.

Casey, K. (1993) *I answer with my life*. New York: Routledge.

Christman, J., Hirshman, J., Holtz, A., Perry, H., Spelkman, R., Williams, M. (1995) Doing Eve's Work: Women Principals write about their practice. In *Anthropology and Education Quarterly*, Vol. 26, No. 2 June 1995.

Goodson, I.F. (ed.) (1992). *Studying Teachers' Lives*. New York: Teachers College Press.

Hyde, K.A.L. and Kadzamira, E.C. (1994) GABLE, Knowledge, Attitudes and Practice Pilot Survey. Report, Centre for Social Research, University of Malawi, Zomba.

Kelly, R. 'Putting emphasis on women cuts no ice with feminists'. In *The Guardian* 21st July 1994, UK.

Langeveld, M.J. (1963) The Psychology of Teachers and the Teaching Profession. In *The Year Book of Education* 1963; the education and training of teachers. London: Evans Bros.

Mac an Ghaill, M. (1994) *The Making of Men: masculinities, sexualities and schooling*. Milton Keynes: Open University Press.

Meena, UNICEF animated film series, production collaboration with Hanna-Barbera Productions and Ram Mohan Studios, Dhaka.

Mishra, A. 'School Teacher Molests Minor'. In *The Utkal Age/The Asian Age* 8th April 1997, India.

Morley, L. and Walsh, V. (eds) (1995) *Feminist Academics: creative agents for change*. London: Taylor and Francis.

Newmark, V. 'Don't mess with the girls'. In *Times Educational Supplement*, 28th February 1997, UK.

Widdowson, F (1983): *Going up into the Next Class*. London: Hutchinson.

Select Bibliography

Aaron, J and Walby, S (1991) (eds.) *Out of the Margins: women's studies in the nineties*. Lewes: Falmer.

Acker, S. ed (1989) *Teachers, Gender and Careers*. Lewes: Falmer Press.

Acker, S. (1994) *Gendered Education: sociological reflections on women, teaching and feminism*. Buckingham: Open University Press.

Adler, S., Laney, J. and Packer, M. (1993) *Managing Women*. Buckingham, Philadelphia: Open University Press.

Anand, A. (1993) *The Power to Change: a report by the Women's Feature* Service. London: Zed.

Appleton, H. (ed.) (1995) *Do It Herself: women and technical innovation*. London: Intermediate Technology.

Ball, S. (ed) (1990) *Foucault and Education*. London: Routledge.

Biklen, S. K. (1995) *School Work: gender and the cultural construction of teaching*. New York: Teachers College Press.

Blancet, T. (1996) *Lost Innocence Stolen Childhood*. Dhaka: The University Press Ltd.

British Broadcasting Corporation (1994) *Breaking Glass*. London: BBC Education.

British Council (1993) *Good Government Development Priorities: Guidelines*. Manchester: The British Council.

Calitz, L.; Viljoen, J.; Moller, T. and van der Bank, A. (1992) *School Management*. Pretoria: Via Afrika Limited.

Cantor, D.W. and Bernay, T. (1992) *Women in Power: the secrets of leadership*. Boston: Houghton Mifflin Company.

Casey, K. (1993) *I answer with my life*. New York: Routledge.

Collins, P.H. (1990) *Black Feminist Thought: knowledge, consciousness and the politics of empowerment*. New York: Routledge.

Davidson, M. and Cooper, C. (1992) *Shattering the Glass Ceiling*. London: Paul Chapman.

Davies, L. (1994) *Beyond Authoritarian School Management: the challenge for transparency*. Ticknall: Education Now.

Davies, L. and Gunawardena, C. (1992) *Women and Men in International Management: the challenge for transparency*. Paris: IIEP.

Davies, L. and Harber, C. (1997) *School Management and Effectiveness in Developing Countries: the post-bureaucratic school*. London: Cassell.

Driscoll, D-M.and Goldberg, C. R. (1993) *Members of the Club: the coming of age of executive women*. New York: The Free Press.

Einhorn, B. (1993) *Cinderella Goes to Market: citizenship, gender and women's movements in East Central Europe*. London: Verso.

Ellis, P. (1990) *Measures increasing the participation of girls and women in technical and vocational education and training: a Caribbean study.* London: Commonwealth Secretariat.

Firth-Cozens, J. and West, M. (eds.) (1991) *Women At Work.* Milton Keynes: Open University Press.

Goodson, I.F. (ed) (1992) *Studying Teachers' Lives.* New York: Teachers College Press.

Gunew, S. (1991) (ed) *A Reader in Feminist Knowledge.* London: Routledge.

Harber, C. (ed) (1995) *Developing Democratic Education.* Ticknall: Education Now.

Harding, J. (1992) *Breaking the Barrier: girls in science education.* Paris: IIEP.

Harrington, M. (1995) *Women Lawyers: rewriting the rules.* New York: Penguin Books.

Helgesen, S. (1995) *The Female Advantage: women's ways of leadership.* New York: Doubleday.

Ianello, K. (1992) *Decisions without hierarchy: feminist interventions in organisation theory and practice.* London: Routledge.

Kelly, R. (1991) *The Gendered Economy.* Newbury Park: Sage Publications Inc.

King, E.M. and Hill M.A. (1993) *Women's Education in Developing Countries: barriers, benefits and policies.* Washington DC: World Bank.

Klein, G. (1993) *Education Towards Race Equality.* London: Cassell.

Mac an Ghaill, M. (1994) *The Making of Men: masculinities, sexualities and schooling.* Buckingham: Open University Press.

Maher, A.F. and Thompson Tetreault, M.K. (1994) *The Feminist Classroom.* New York: Basic Books.

McCormick, T.M. (1994) *Creating the Nonsexist Classroom: a multicultural approach.* New York: Teachers College Press.

Mellin-Olsen, S. (1996) (ed) *Women's Mathematics Education Talk.* Norway: Caspar Forlag.

Morley, L and Walsh, V. (eds) (1995) *Feminist Academics: creative agents for change.* London: Taylor and Francis.

Nichols, N.A. (ed) (1994) *Reach For the Top: women and the changed facts of work life.* Boston: Harvard Business School Publishing Corporation.

Odaga, A. and Heneveld, W. (1995) *Girls and Schools in Sub-Saharan Africa: from analysis to action.* World Bank Technical Paper Number 298. Washington DC: World Bank.

Olson, G.A. and Hirsh, E. (eds.) (1995) *Women Writing Culture.* New York: Suny.

Ouston, J. (ed) (1993) *Women in Education Management.* Harlow: Longman.

Ozga, J. (ed) (1993) *Women in Educational Management.* Buckingham: Open University Press.

Ramphele, M. (1995) *A Life.* Cape Town and Johannesburg: David Philip.

Rogers, A. (1994) *Women, Literacy, Income Generation.* Reading: Education for Development.

Said, E. (1996) *Representations of the Intellectual.* Vintage Books: New York.

Sarup, M. (1993) *An Introductory Guide to Post-Structuralism and Postmodernism.* The University of Georgia Press: Athens, USA.

Simillie, I. (1997) *Words & Deeds,* BRAC at 25. Dhaka: BRAC.

Siraj-Blatchford, I. (ed) (1993) *Race, Gender and the Education of Teachers.* Buckingham: Open University Press.

Spender, D. (1995) *Nattering on the Net: women, power and cyberspace.* Melbourne: Spinifex.

Stromquist, N. (1994) *Gender and Basic Education in International Development Cooperation.* New York: UNICEF.

Suryardarma, M. (1993) *Indonesian Women in Higher Education Management.* UNESCO.

Swainson, N. (1996) *Redressing Gender Inequalities in Education: a review of constraints and priorities in Malawi, Zambia and Zimbabwe.* Report to The British Development Division in Central Africa of the Overseas Development Administration.

UNICEF *Meena* animated film series, produced in collaboration with Hanna-Berbera productions and Ram Mohan Studios. Dhaka.

Vinnicombe, S. and Colwill, N.L. (1995) *The Essence of Women in Management.* UK: Prentice Hall Int'l (UK) Ltd.

United Nations (1995) *The World's Women: trends and statistics.* New York: United Nations.

Weber, S. and Mitchell, C. (1995) *That's Funny You Don't Look Like a Teacher: interrogating images and identity in popular culture.* Lewes: Falmer Press.

White, K (1996) *Why good girls don't get ahead but gutsy girls do.* New York: Warner Books.

World Bank (1991) *Vocational and Technical Education and Training: a World Bank policy paper.* Washington DC: World Bank.

World Bank (1995) *Priorities and Strategies for Education: a World Bank review.* Washington DC: World Bank.

WCEFA (1990) *World Conference on Education for All: Meeting Basic Learning Needs* 5-9 March 1990, Jomtien, Thailand. Final Report. New York: Inter-agency Commission, WCEFA.

Index